FIFA WORLD CUP
Qatar2022™

Published in 2022 under licence by Welbeck, an imprint of Welbeck Non-Fiction Limited, part of the Welbeck Publishing Group.
Based in London and Sydney.

www.welbeckpublishing.com

ISBN 978-1-78739-988-4

10 9 8 7 6 5 4 3 2 1

Printed in Dubai.

Editors: Ross Hamilton & Conor Kilgallon
Design Manager: Russell Knowles
Design: RockJaw Creative
Picture Research: Paul Langan
Production: Rachel Burgess

The facts and stats in this book are correct as of May 2022.

FIFA WORLD CUP
Qatar2022™

THE OFFICIAL GUIDE

KEIR RADNEDGE

CONTENTS

◆ ·◆· ◆ ◆ ◆ ◆ ·◆·

FIFA WORLD CUP
Qatar2022™

© FIFA TM

INTRODUCTION

The year 2022 is a unique one in the annals of the FIFA World Cup™ and of the global game itself. For the first time, the greatest event in association football, the most widely followed sporting extravaganza on the planet, will take place in the Arab world.

ABOVE: The official FIFA World Cup ball sits in front of the Doha skyline in the run-up to the final draw on 1 April 2022.

Not only that, but the versatility of football will see the Gulf state of Qatar hosting the finals in the northern hemisphere winter rather than the traditional June/July dates. The proposal, when it was raised first, provoked widespread debate but, in becoming reality, is evidence of football's unity of purpose and imagination.

Qatar itself has been independent for only 50 years and local fans' love of football has never been in any doubt. Without that commitment it would not have been possible to build such a stunning collection of new and redeveloped stadiums in which to welcome the world's top national teams, their officials, the media and supporters.

The FIFA World Cup™ is 92 years old and keeps on strengthening its attraction. Some 13 teams competed in Uruguay in 1930. Now, 32 teams will compete in Qatar and a further expansion will see 48 teams enjoy a unique tournament in Canada, Mexico and the USA in four years' time – the first edition to be hosted across three countries. As the President of FIFA, Gianni Infantino has said: "The whole world deserves to have the World Cup."

The FIFA World Cup Qatar 2022™ finals will be a triumph for the international football family over the worldwide crisis created by the COVID-19 pandemic over the past three years. FIFA, the six continental confederations and its 211 member associations found ways and means to work within the essential security and travel restrictions imposed across the world.

The complex qualifying competition was carried through to its conclusion in Africa, Asia, Europe, Oceania and North, South and Central America.

ABOVE: The FIFA World Cup trophy on display in the Doha Exhibition Center.

Old favourites and new forces in football will share the adventure in Qatar, which has been building up to these finals ever since the original hosting award in December 2010.

France will be back to defend the World Cup, which they lifted for a second time in Russia four years ago, after defeating Croatia in Moscow in the first final to see the use of video assistant referees. Most of the other previous World Cup victors will be chasing them down.

Brazil are the record five-time champions, who are impatient to regain

their place on the podium for the first time since winning in 2002 in Japan and Korea Republic. Germany, with four titles to their name, are focused on trying to equal the Brazilians' record. South American members of this unique club include Argentina and Uruguay, who each triumphed twice. European World Cup history is represented by England, champions as hosts back in 1966, and Spain, winners in 2010 in South Africa.

The only former champions watching from afar will be Italy, who were eliminated in the European qualifying play-offs.

At one time, football's leaders were concerned that national-team football was fighting a losing battle against the club game. Instead, the ever-increasing popularity of the World Cup and the creation of a string of other national-team competitions around the globe has proved quite the opposite.

Proof is to be found in the over-subscribed stampede for tickets among all those fans around the world who want to be present to see history made in Qatar in November and December 2022.

FIFA WORLD CUP
Qatar2022™

WELCOME TO QATAR

Qatar has waited longer than any other prospective host of the FIFA World Cup for the excitement and glory of welcoming the football world to the sport's greatest showpiece. Finally, 12 years after Qatar was awarded the hosting rights, November and December 2022 will see the long-awaited duels between rivals old and new in the Middle East for the first time in the tournament's 92-year history.

ALL EYES ON QATAR

The FIFA World Cup Qatar 2022 will be the most widely followed of all time. Fans all around the planet will focus their attention, via every form of modern communications technology, on the games and goals guaranteed to write a new chapter in football history.

FIFA WORLD CUP Qatar2022™

With a population of 2.9m and an area of 11,571km², Qatar will be the smallest nation ever to stage the FIFA World Cup, beating the previous record held by 1930 host Uruguay, with its population of 3.5m and an area of 176,000km².

The benefits deriving from Qatar's rapid and innovative development since achieving independence from British protectorate status in 1971 will help to ensure that all the essential logistical building blocks are in place for the unique November kick-off.

This is the first FIFA World Cup to be staged in the northern-hemisphere winter, for reasons of health. Players, officials and fans will therefore be

protected from the risks they may otherwise have faced due to the local high temperatures in the traditional FIFA World Cup months of June and July. Qatar will also be the first country – apart from inaugural host Uruguay in 1930 – to welcome the world without having previously appeared at the final tournament.

World football's governing body, FIFA, was founded in 1904 by representatives from seven countries: Belgium, Denmark, France, the Netherlands, Spain, Sweden and Switzerland. FIFA's membership now totals 211 member associations that are all also members of one of the six confederations representing the

regions into which the world is divided for this purpose: CAF (Africa), the AFC (Asia), UEFA (Europe), Concacaf (North and Central America and the Caribbean), the OFC (Oceania) and CONMEBOL (South America).

The founding meeting was held in Paris, where FIFA was headquartered until moving to Switzerland in the 1930s. Significantly, one of FIFA's first decisions was to secure the right to organise an international championship. The historic first edition of this tournament took place in Uruguay in 1930.

The FIFA World Cup has been staged every four years in peacetime since then. The game's steady rise has

WeL

been evidenced in the staging plans, both for this year and for the next decade. Some 32 national teams will contest the final tournament in Qatar. The growing popularity of the game will then see the tournament expand to include 48 teams in four years' time at the first edition to be hosted across three countries, namely Canada, Mexico and the USA.

Naturally, all of FIFA's 211 member associations want to be present at the party. This requires a complex qualification system that was made even more challenging by the effects of the COVID-19 pandemic. The first goal in the qualifiers for the 2022 tournament was scored all the way back on 6 June 2019, when Norjmoogiin Tsedenbal got on the scoresheet after nine minutes of Mongolia's 2-0 win over Brunei Darussalam in an Asian first-round encounter.

This is the 22nd final tournament. Qatar follows in the proud footsteps of previous hosts Uruguay, Italy (twice), France (twice), Brazil (twice), Switzerland, Sweden, Chile, England, Mexico (twice), Germany (twice), Argentina, Spain, the USA, Japan and Korea Republic jointly, South Africa and Russia.

Only eight nations have scaled the pinnacle of ultimate success: Brazil (five times), Italy and Germany (four times each), Uruguay, Argentina and France (twice apiece), England and Spain.

Qatar has had more time to prepare than any previous FIFA World Cup host. FIFA launched a joint bidding process for both the 2018 and 2022 final tournaments in January 2009. Ultimately, it was agreed that Europe should focus on 2018 and the rest of the world on 2022. The five candidates to stage the latter tournament were Australia, Japan, Qatar, Korea Republic and the USA.

Both World Cups were awarded by the then FIFA Executive Committee in Zurich on 2 December 2010, with the hosting rights going to Russia for 2018 and to Qatar for 2022. In July 2018, FIFA and the Qatari authorities agreed that the 2022 tournament should be staged in November and December rather than June and July. This was in response to health concerns for players and fans considering the summer heat in the region.

All 64 matches will be played in the 28 days between 21 November and 18 December (inclusive), making it the shortest FIFA World Cup final tournament since 1978. The format remains the same as the one introduced in 1998. A group stage featuring eight groups of four nations will be followed by a direct-elimination knockout stage with a round of 16, quarter-finals, semi-finals, third-place play-off and final.

Qatar has been hosting global football championships since 1995, when it stepped in at short notice to stage the FIFA World Youth Championship (now the FIFA U-20 World Cup™). Since then, it has welcomed the FIFA Club World Cup™ in 2019 and 2020, and the FIFA Arab Cup™ in November and December 2021. Several of the World Cup venues, described as "fantastic" by FIFA President Gianni Infantino, were used for the Arab Cup.

All eyes will now be on hosts Qatar as they kick off their campaign for the historic FIFA World Cup 2022™ against Ecuador at the Al Bayt Stadium in Al Khor.

BELOW: The magnificent vista of the rapidly expanding Doha, the central focus of the finals.

FIFA WORLD CUP Qatar2022™

THE STADIUMS

Qatar has eight FIFA World Cup 2022 stadiums spread across the country – but none are more than an hour away from one another, so there's no need for flights or long-distance trains. Fans can even attend two matches in one day. That's what a truly compact tournament looks like.

Seven of the stadiums have been built from scratch while one, Khalifa International Stadium, has been completely refurbished. The iconic venue, embedded in the hearts of all Qataris and the region's rich football culture, was destined for the FIFA World Cup 2022.

Culture is a significant theme across every stadium. Each new venue has been designed in tribute to Qatar's rich traditions, heritage and location – offering fans a unique world of discovery.

In keeping with Qatar's commitment to host the most sustainable FIFA World Cup ever, all were innovatively designed and constructed in ways that can inspire future sporting events around the world. And, after the last ball has been kicked, over 200,000 stadium seats will be donated to countries in need of sporting infrastructure.

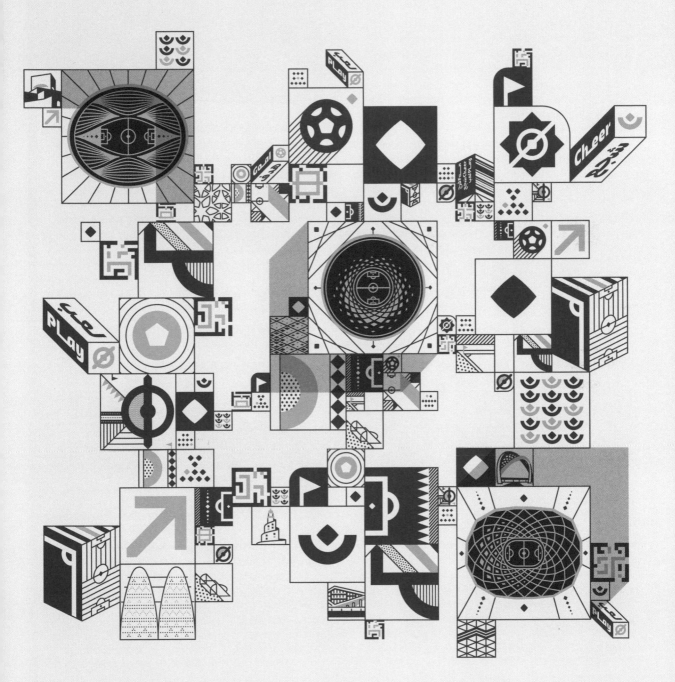

Al Bayt Stadium
Enjoy the warmest of Arab welcomes
- 60,000-capacity arena
- Traditional nomadic tent design
- Host of the FIFA World Cup Qatar 2022 opening match
- **CITY:** Al Khor

Al Bayt Stadium's role as host for the FIFA World Cup 2022 opening match was assured from its very first design sketch. Qatar turned to the rich fabric of its culture and traditions to welcome the world in the most authentic way – warmly inviting guests into comfort as custom has demanded in this part of the world for centuries.

Inspired by the *bayt al sha'ar* of Qatar's nomadic peoples, the stadium's magnificent tent structure envelopes an ultra-modern football stadium. Traditionally, the tents could be identified by black and white stripes. This is faithfully reflected on the arena's distinctive exterior, as are the vibrant *sadu* patterns that greet fans once inside. The design is also practical; shade provided by the structure and its retractable roof system complement the stadium's advanced cooling technologies without using any additional power.

With sustainability and best energy usage at the forefront of Al Bayt Stadium's development, the venue's modular construction allows the upper tier to be removed after the tournament. This means almost half of the 60,000 seats will be donated to developing nations across the world. The project extends to the surrounding city of Al Khor where the numerous parks, lakes and protected green belt land stretch out from the stadium to the sea – ensuring a lasting legacy from the world's most welcoming stadium.

Stadium 974
A big win for innovation and sustainability
- 40,000-capacity arena
- Constructed from shipping containers and modular steel
- Design echoes the nearby port and Doha's maritime history
- **CITY:** Doha

History is more than an account of past events; it is something alive. And, in the case of Stadium 974, it is being made right now. Constructed entirely from certified shipping containers and modular steel, this innovative FIFA World Cup 2022 sporting venue uniquely shows Qatar's unwavering commitment to cost-effective sustainability and daring design.

The stadium pays tribute to Qatar's traditions of worldwide trade and seafaring. 974 is the international dialing code for Qatar, as well as the exact number of shipping containers used in its construction. Situated in the portside area and in sight of Doha's spectacular coastal cityscape, 40,000 fans will instantly feel the cool breeze as it rolls in over the gentle waters of the Arabian Gulf.

After the tournament, the stadium will be dismantled for repurposing. Seats will be donated, while containers and super-structure material will be used across a range of non-sporting projects. A verdant waterfront development boasting fabulous facilities for the local community will also spring to life, as well as a dynamic hub for trade and business. This new concept in venue development ensures that while Stadium 974's physical presence may be temporary – its legacy will live forever.

Sta

Al Thumama Stadium
A coming of age for the beautiful game

- 40,000-capacity arena
- Design represents the *gahfiya*, a traditional hat worn across the Middle East
- The only completely circular FIFA World Cup Qatar 2022 stadium
- **CITY:** Doha

Dynamic and truly imaginative, Al Thumama Stadium's design is in keeping with all of Qatar's new FIFA World Cup 2022 stadiums. The arena has been designed to celebrate local culture and traditions just as much as the tournament itself. But this stadium's meaning tugs at the hearts of locals and resonates across the region just that little bit more.

Its bold, circular form reflects the *gahfiya* – the traditional woven cap adorned by men and boys all across the Middle East. An integral part of family life and central to traditions, the *gahfiya* symbolises the coming of age for youth, a time of emerging self-confidence and individual ambition that marks their first steps into the future and a realisation of dreams.

For many, the first sighting of this magnificent stadium will come from above as flights descend into Hamad International Airport. The venue's unmistakeable presence stands out majestically amid its lush green surroundings. Areas for play and relaxation not only enhance the venue but also the lives of families in the community. Al Thumama Stadium brings meaning beyond its inspiration and purpose – it marks a coming of age for the beautiful game.

Ahmad Bin Ali Stadium
Where desert stories unfold

- 40,000-capacity arena
- Located in one of Qatar's most traditional cities
- Home to the hugely popular Al Rayyan Sports Club
- **CITY:** Al Rayyan

Ahmad Bin Ali Stadium stands proudly in Al Rayyan, one Qatar's most historic cities and home to the famous Al-Rayyan SC. Fittingly, this magnificent arena will see football's heroes write their names into history beside an enchanting desert landscape that is imbued with legendary Qatari tales. Naturally, these stories are held close to the hearts of the locals – a warm and welcoming people who love their football just as much as their fascinating past.

In keeping with other FIFA World Cup Qatar 2022 venues, Ahmad Bin Ali Stadium's design and that of its surrounding buildings mirrors aspects of the local culture and traditions. The intricate façade reflects the sweeping undulations of the nearby sand dunes. Beautiful geometric patterns characterise different aspects of the country, such as the importance of family, the beauty of the desert, native flora and fauna, as well as local and international trade.

The stadium will become Al-Rayyan SC's home ground when the tournament ends. More than 80% of the construction materials came from the original stadium that occupied this site – with all new materials selected for their sustainable qualities. Even the trees that surrounded the original venue were carefully retained for future replanting. If you're visiting, you'll be able to travel via an environmentally friendly new metro system – complementing a truly sustainable venue.

Khalifa International Stadium

A sporting legend re-energised

- 40,000-capacity arena
- Adored by many as the home of football in Qatar
- Built in 1976 and transformed for the FIFA World Cup Qatar 2022
- **CITY:** Al Rayyan

Khalifa International Stadium's proud list of sporting events have secured it a unique place in the hearts of Qataris. Since 1976, the big moments have found a home here time and time again. In fact, you cannot mention football or athletics in Qatar without referring to this iconic venue. As a reward for years of service, the stadium received a complete refit for the FIFA World Cup Qatar 2022.

The stadium's reopening was cause for much celebration in May 2017 when it brought to life its spectacular inauguration ceremony as host of the Amir Cup final – the showpiece event of Qatar's most precious cup. It was quite something as an old friend returned to youthful glory. Its most recognisable features were always its dual arches – these remain intact, with a wide canopy now stretched out below them. This complements the stadium's cooling system to maintain a comfortable temperature throughout the arena.

As a previous stage for the Arabian Gulf Cup, the FIFA Club World Cup and IAAF World Athletics Championships, Khalifa International Stadium is ready to welcome the world for the FIFA World Cup Qatar 2022. The new tier added 12,000 seats to increase capacity to 40,000, while the addition of digital lighting and a beautiful new façade ensures Khalifa International Stadium will continue to sparkle long into the future.

Al Janoub Stadium
See football sail into a new era

- 40,000-capacity arena
- In the southern city of Al Wakrah, one of Qatar's oldest continuously inhabited areas
- Design pays tribute to the city's seafaring past
- **CITY:** Al Wakrah

Al Janoub Stadium lies in the southern city of Al Wakrah, one of Qatar's oldest continuously inhabited areas. It is a city with a rich history but one that also has its sights set firmly on a new horizon – the future of football. As the FIFA World Cup Qatar 2022 plays out, the world will be invited into some of the most unique stadiums ever built for the beautiful game. Al Janoub Stadium sits firmly in that category.

The stadium's visionary shape can be attributed to the legendary architect Zaha Hadid's company that was charged with the design. Perfectly reflecting the wind-filled sails of traditional dhow boats, it pays tribute to Al Wakrah's maritime past of fishing and pearl diving. For centuries, these craft worked the Gulf waters and beyond, then returned to Al Wakrah's port laden with the sea's bounty.

After the tournament, Al Janoub Stadium will become a new home for sport and entertainment in southern Qatar. Its capacity will be reduced to 20,000, guaranteeing an electric atmosphere for local side Al-Wakrah SC's matches. Beyond football, the long-term benefits of the venue's legacy include a school, a wedding hall, cycling, horse riding and running tracks, restaurants, marketplaces, gyms and parkland. The future sails well behind this wonderful arena.

Education City Stadium
Bringing football and knowledge together

- 40,000-capacity arena
- Surrounded by some of Qatar's leading universities
- Design reflects a diamond in the desert
- **CITY:** Al Rayyan

Education City Stadium shines a brilliant light on Qatar's position as a dynamic learning hub for students and academics across the region. Its namesake location Education City is a vibrant centre of knowledge. Dotted with leading universities, the corridors buzz with cutting-edge research and new ideas expressing the latest talent and innovations.

The stadium's ultra-modern design fuses with traditional Islamic architecture. On the exterior, triangles create complex diamond-like geometrical patterns that sparkle as the sun moves across the sky. At night you can enjoy a completely different light show as the façade digitally illuminates – putting on the most remarkable performance of all.

Around the campuses, you will discover many first-in-class sporting facilities. After the tournament, more amenities will be added to the stadium precinct, keeping the academic community stimulated away from the classroom.

Lusail Stadium
Alive with culture, an icon for the future

- 80,000-capacity arena
- Centrepiece of Lusail City: a state-of-the-art metropolis
- Host of the FIFA World Cup Qatar 2022 final
- **CITY:** Lusail

Lusail Stadium can be thought of as a cultural icon even before hosting the FIFA World Cup Qatar 2022 final – the event that will secure its place in football and architectural history. Immense yet exquisite, Lusail Stadium's scale and splendour are a wonder and in harmony with its surroundings while providing inspiration far beyond.

The stadium's design reflects the bowls, vessels and other crafted art pieces found all across the Arab and Islamic world during the rise of civilisation in the region. Interplays of light mirror the *fanar* lanterns of the region. With the passing of time, its muted golden exterior will inspire an image of aged metal handicrafts, making it a venue alive with cultural character.

On 18 December, 80,000 fans will come together here for the most unique FIFA World Cup final ever – the first in the Arab world. Afterwards, and in keeping with Qatar's dedication to sustainable development, Lusail Stadium will be transformed into a community space including schools, shops, cafés, sporting facilities and health clinics. This is the amazing we have all been waiting for – it's here, it's now and forever.

Lega

FIFA WORLD CUP
Qatar2022™

THE ROAD
TO QATAR

Over the years, fans in Qatar have enjoyed
fleeting visits from many of the world's
finest footballers for friendly matches and
international events. Now, the smallest country
to host the FIFA World Cup will welcome the
most outstanding national teams who have
triumphed in qualifying campaigns across the
game's six regional confederations.

QUALIFIERS: EUROPE

European football pride at the FIFA World Cup finals will be represented by 13 nations. The ten qualifying groups were wrapped up last November with the table-topping national teams guaranteed the right to bringing their finest players and fans to the finals in Qatar. The runners-up had to wait for the spring and early summer to contest the three remaining slots via the drama of direct elimination play-offs.

The European qualifying format was originally approved by the Executive Committee of European confederation UEFA in December 2019, with the draw taking place one year later. Matches kicked off in March 2021, before the schedule on the international match calendar was disrupted by the effects of the COVID-19 pandemic.

October 2021 saw Germany and then Denmark become the first European national teams to reach the final tournament. Germany became the first Qatar-bound nation, with a decisive 4-0 victory against North Macedonia in Group J. Former England youth international Jamal Musiala scored the last goal as Germany reached the final tournament for the 20th time, with two games to spare.

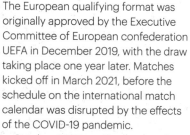

The following day, Denmark followed suit by defeating Austria 1-0 in Copenhagen in Group F. Denmark, semi-finalists in UEFA EURO 2020, owed their victory to a second-half goal from Joakim Mæhle.

This left eight further groups to be decided within a dramatic week of national-team football in November 2021.

Belgium, the FIFA/Coca-Cola World Ranking leaders, secured Group E victory and their place in Qatar with a 3-1 win over Estonia. Wales subsequently took the runners-up spot to enter the play-offs. They were accompanied by the Czech Republic, who finished third. The Czechs benefited from the UEFA Nations League option along with Austria, who had finished

fourth behind Denmark, an improving Scotland and Israel in Group F.

In Group D, world champions France followed Belgium's example. Kylian Mbappé celebrated his first international hat-trick in 32 minutes in an 8-0 victory over Kazakhstan. Karim Benzema scored twice. Mbappé, a key figure in 2018, said: "Even for those of us fortunate enough to have won a World Cup, it's still the ultimate dream to play there."

In Group B, Spain became the fifth European team to qualify when a lone late goal from Álvaro Morata consigned Sweden to the play-offs. Goalkeeper Robin Olsen had tipped Dani Olmo's shot on to the crossbar, but Morata tapped home the rebound and Luis Enrique's men qualified for a 12th consecutive final tournament.

That same evening, the Group A script took an unexpected twist for Spain's Iberian neighbours Portugal. They needed a home draw against Serbia and were doing enough even when Renato Sanches's opener was cancelled out by a Dušan Tadić equaliser. However, half-time substitute Aleksandar Mitrović headed a dramatic late winner to send Serbia to the finals and Portugal into the play-offs.

Defeat ended Portugal's unbroken winning run in home World Cup qualifiers stretching back to October 2013.

LEFT: Spain's Álvaro Morata shoots before Sweden's Victor Lindelöf can tackle.

ABOVE: Serbia's Aleksandar Mitrović celebrates his crucial winning goal against Portugal.

In Group H, Croatia, runners-up in Russia in 2018, overtook the last World Cup hosts with a 1-0 victory in Split. Defender Fedor Kudryashov deflected a cross from Borna Sosa into his own net when the Russian team were only nine minutes from a place in the finals. Their consolation in defeat was a place in the play-offs.

The next 24 hours saw disappointment for Italy after a goalless Group C draw in their World Cup jinx city of Belfast. A defeat there had previously seen Italy miss the 1958 FIFA World Cup™ finals. This time, a 0-0 draw at least provided a play-off place. Switzerland overtook Italy to top the table by defeating Bulgaria 4-0.

The Netherlands secured their place with a 2-0 Group G home win over Norway with late goals from Steven Bergwijn and Memphis Depay. Coach Louis van Gaal, who led the Dutch to a third-place finish in 2014, had to watch from a wheelchair in the stands after injuring a hip falling off his bicycle the previous weekend.

Defeat was costly for a Norway team missing injured Erling Braut Haaland. The play-off spot was instead taken by Turkey.

England wrapped up their Group I campaign with a 5-0 victory at home to Albania and a 10-0 win away to San Marino. Captain Harry Kane's late surge of a hat-trick against Albania and a four-goal haul against San Marino meant that he finished as 12-goal joint top scorer in the European section, along with Depay. They were followed, on eight goals each, by Israel's Eran Zahavi, Poland captain Robert Lewandowski and Serbia's Aleksandar Mitrović.

The European teams certain to qualify were therefore group winners Serbia, Spain, Switzerland, France, Belgium, Denmark, the Netherlands, Croatia, England and Germany. Play-off opportunities remained for group runners-up Portugal, Sweden, Italy, Ukraine, Wales, Scotland, Turkey, Russia, Poland and North Macedonia. They were joined by the Czech Republic and Austria, courtesy of their UEFA Nations League status.

RIGHT: Netherlands' Memphis Depay bursts clear of Turkey's Yusuf Yazıcı in Istanbul.

QUALIFIERS: CONMEBOL

The South American qualifying path for the FIFA World Cup is one of the most intense and demanding before four nations know for certain that they will be present at the finals. The route involves all ten member nations of CONMEBOL, the continental confederation, playing each other both home and away.

Many of the players earn their living with clubs in Europe and some even further afield. This means travel logistics are complex at the best of times and the worldwide COVID-19 pandemic meant that these were among the worst of times.

Traditionally, since no draw for mini-leagues is necessary, the CONMEBOL qualifying phase begins 15 months after the final of the previous World Cup. However, the pandemic saw a series of postponements and rearrangements approved and coordinated through FIFA and CONMEBOL, with competition kicking off in empty stadiums only on 20 October 2020.

Uruguay's Luis Suárez scored the first goal of the tournament in a 2-1 victory over Chile in the historic Estadio Centenario in Montevideo. Suárez was an appropriate man to open the drama. He had opened the group scoring in both 2010 and 2014, while Uruguay team-mate Martín Cáceres had celebrated the initial goal in South America's 2018 FIFA World Cup™ qualifying tournament.

Brazil and Argentina were the obvious favourites to qualify for the right to play in Qatar, but competition was guaranteed from such proud old rivals as Chile and Uruguay. In fact, only one South American national team have never reached the finals:

Venezuela. This speaks volumes for the intensity of the action.

Coach Tite's Brazil began confidently with a 5-0 home victory over Bolivia in São Paulo, inspired by two goals from the Liverpool forward Roberto Firmino. Argentina had more problems in defeating Ecuador by the minimum margin of 1-0, secured by an early penalty from captain Leo Messi. Ecuador would ultimately see both their talent and character vindicated when they achieved qualification for the finals themselves.

Quickly, Brazil established command at the top of the table. The record five-time World Cup winners won all of their first seven consecutive matches before hosting their great southern rivals, Argentina. The occasion proved an anti-climax when the match was abandoned in the opening minutes over concerns raised by local health authority officials.

Brazil picked up where they left off with two more victories before dropping their first points in a goalless draw in Colombia. They reasserted themselves with a victory over Uruguay and then a home victory over Colombia, which confirmed their qualification for Qatar with a remarkable five matchdays still to play, plus the rearranged fixture with Argentina. The Lyon forward Lucas Paquetá scored the all-important goal, which guaranteed that Brazil would maintain their record as the only nation

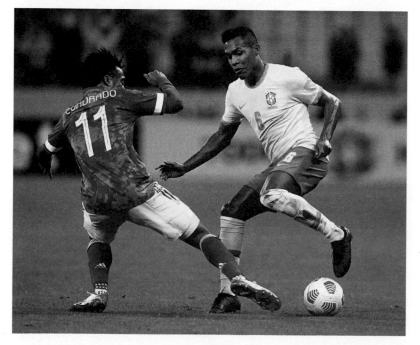

LEFT: Brazil's Alex Sandro outwits Colombia's Juan Cuadrado in São Paulo.

ABOVE: Peru's Luis Advíncula and Gianluca Lapadula lead the celebrations after beating Paraguay to reach the play-offs.

to play in every edition of the World Cup finals.

Five days later, Argentina followed Brazil's example. They qualified for Qatar themselves by securing the necessary point with a goalless draw at home to Brazil in San Juan.

A four-month hiatus followed before Uruguay and Ecuador secured their own spots in Qatar in March of this year. Uruguay beat Peru 1-0 and Ecuador lost 3-1 to Paraguay, meaning both teams had reached 25 points with one match to play and out of reach of Peru on 21 points in fifth place: Uruguay and Ecuador had battled through difficult routes in which both teams lost six games each.

The Uruguayans even finished with a balanced goals record of 22 scored and 22 conceded.

Kick-off for the concluding matchday saw Peru with 21 points and Colombia with 20 and both with a chance of reaching the play-offs. Peru knew that victory at home to Paraguay was essential. First-half goals from Gianluca Lapadula and Yoshimar Yotún delivered the 2-0 victory, which rendered Colombia's 1-0 win in Venezuela in vain. The Peruvians, finalists in Russia in 2018, thus went forward to the draw for the intercontinental play-offs.

Completion of the group saw 223 goals having been scored in

89 matches, with the exception of the Brazil-Argentina tie, which FIFA had ordered to be rearranged. Bolivia failed to qualify but had the consolation of seeing captain and all-time top scorer Marcelo Moreno finish as leading marksman in the mini-league with ten goals. Moreno was born in Bolivia, but his father was Brazilian, so he played for Brazil at U-18 and U-20 levels before opting for Bolivia, his mother's country, at senior level.

Second place among the qualifying marksmen was shared by Brazil's Neymar and Uruguay's Suárez with eight goals apiece, followed by Argentina's Messi and Lautaro Martínez on seven each.

QUALIFIERS: REST OF THE WORLD

The race to join hosts Qatar in the finals began in June 2019. Completion of qualifying action was a logistical triumph, considering COVID-19 pandemic complications. Europe and South America shared 17 certain slots, which left everything to play for in Africa, Asia, Central and North America, and Oceania.

AFRICA

All 54 African members of FIFA entered the CAF qualifying section, which opened with a knockout tournament between the lowest-placed nations in the FIFA/Coca-Cola World Ranking. The winners entered a second round group stage, whose fallers included Côte d'Ivoire, World Cup finalists three times between 2006 and 2014, and South Africa, hosts in 2010.

Côte d'Ivoire were runners-up in Group D behind Cameroon, while

Bafana Bafana lost out to Ghana in Group G by the slimmest margin. Both finished with 13 points and a plus-four goal difference, but Ghana had scored seven goals compared with South Africa's six.

The third round featured five knockout ties, with the winners heading to Qatar. Morocco had few problems defeating Congo DR 5-2 on aggregate and fellow North Africans Tunisia defeated Mali 1-0. Ghana, however, needed the rulebook again. This time the away goals rule edged them past Nigeria after a 0-0

stalemate in Kumasi and then a 1-1 draw in Abuja. Midfielder Thomas Partey struck the all-important away goal.

Away goals also brought Cameroon victory over Algeria, despite losing the first leg 1-0 at home in Douala. Cameroon levelled on aggregate in Blida, with a goal from Jean-Eric Choupo-Moting earning extra time. Algeria thought they had reached Qatar when left-winger Ahmed Touba scored in the 118th minute, but Cameroon hit back with a crucial winner from Lyon forward Toko Ekambi in the fourth minute of stoppage time.

Star forwards Sadio Mané and Mohamed Salah from Liverpool in the English Premier League confronted each other in the remaining tie, between Senegal and Egypt. The tie was expected to be tight after Senegal defeated Egypt on penalties in the Africa Cup of Nations final seven weeks earlier.

Egypt won 1-0 in Cairo and Senegal won by the same margin after extra time in Dakar. Again, a shoot-out proved decisive and Senegal could celebrate. Salah shot Egypt's first kick over the bar and Mané converted the last penalty to send Senegal into the finals.

ABOVE: Egypt's Mohamed Salah (left) closes down Senegal's Sadio Mané, his Liverpool team-mate, during their showdown in Cairo.

ASIA

All 46 of the AFC's FIFA member associations set out on the road to Qatar, including the hosts of the finals. This was because the first two rounds also doubled up in the qualifying system for the 2023 AFC Asian Cup.

The first round featured six knockout ties, before the second round groups meant the end of the line for Kuwait and Bahrain, both previous World Cup finalists. Syria were notable winners of Group A ahead of China PR, whose consolation was to progress as one of the runners-up with the best records.

Two groups of six teams made up the third round with the top two teams going to Qatar and third-placed teams contesting a regional play-off. Group A saw IR Iran and Korea Republic finish well clear of the rest of the field, while Saudi Arabia and Japan led the way from Group B. Australia started well but never recovered lost ground after a dip in form brought defeat in Japan and successive dropped points from draws against Saudi Arabia and China PR.

Australia and the United Arab Emirates were left to contest the right to a place in the intercontinental play-offs.

Concacaf

The decisive group stage of the Concacaf qualifying section was played out between September 2021 and March this year after delays, postponements and reorganisation enforced by the fall-out from the COVID-19 pandemic.

The five best-placed teams in the FIFA/Coca-Cola World Ranking – Mexico, the USA, Costa Rica, Jamaica and Honduras – had all been awarded byes to the third round. They were joined from the second round by El Salvador, Canada and Panama. The trio had won both their initial groups and then home-and-away ties against Saint Kitts and Nevis, Haiti and Curaçao respectively.

Mexico and the USA were the World Cup heavyweights with a total of 27 appearances at the finals between them, but they did not have it all their own way.

Instead, Canada, who will share with them joint hosting of the 2026 finals, emerged to win the group on goal

ABOVE: Tajon Buchanan celebrates Canada's second goal in the 4–0 win over Jamaica, which sent them to the finals.

difference, ahead of *El Tri*. The USA needed a superior goal difference to secure the third and last secure slot at the finals ahead of Costa Rica. Canadian forward Cyle Larin was the group's leading marksman with six goals, one more than team-mate Jonathan David and the USA's Christian Pulisic.

OCEANIA

The immediate challenge for members of the Oceania confederation was to reach their own tournament final with the prize beyond that being entry into the intercontinental play-offs. The logistical complications created by the worldwide COVID-19 pandemic eventually led the Oceania confederation to schedule a centralised tournament in Qatar.

Tonga, American Samoa and Samoa all withdrew before the tournament, while Vanuatu and the Cook Islands both pulled out after the tournament had kicked off. The Solomon Islands defeated Tahiti in the only tie in Group A, while New Zealand won all their matches in Group B. New Zealand followed up by defeating the Solomon Islands 5-0 in the final in Doha to reach the intercontinental play-offs.

FIFA WORLD CUP Qatar 2022™

AFRICA (CAF)

SECOND ROUND

Teams	P	W	D	D	GF	GA	Pts
GROUP A							
Algeria	6	4	2	0	25	4	14
Burkina Faso	6	3	3	0	12	4	12
Niger	6	2	1	3	13	17	7
Djibouti	6	0	0	6	4	29	0
GROUP B							
Tunisia	6	4	1	1	11	2	13
Eq. Guinea	6	3	2	1	6	5	11
Zambia	6	2	1	3	8	9	7
Mauritania	6	0	2	4	2	11	2
GROUP C							
Nigeria	6	4	1	1	9	3	13
Cabo Verde	6	3	2	1	8	6	11
Liberia	6	2	0	4	5	8	6
Cen. Afr. Rep.	6	1	1	4	4	9	4
GROUP D							
Cameroon	6	5	0	1	12	3	15
Côte d'Ivoire	6	4	1	1	10	3	13
Mozambique	6	1	1	4	2	8	4
Malawi	6	1	0	5	2	12	3
GROUP E							
Mali	6	5	1	0	11	0	16
Uganda	6	2	3	1	3	2	9
Kenya	6	1	3	2	4	9	6
Rwanda	6	0	1	5	2	9	1

Teams	P	W	D	D	GF	GA	Pts
GROUP F							
Egypt	6	4	2	0	10	4	14
Gabon	6	2	1	3	7	8	7
Libya	6	2	1	3	4	7	7
Angola	6	1	2	3	6	8	5
GROUP G							
Ghana	6	4	1	1	7	3	13
South Africa	6	4	1	1	6	2	13
Ethiopia	6	1	2	3	4	7	5
Zimbabwe	6	0	2	4	2	7	2
GROUP H							
Senegal	6	5	1	0	15	4	16
Togo	6	2	2	2	5	6	8
Namibia	6	1	2	3	5	10	5
Congo	6	0	3	3	5	10	3
GROUP I							
Morocco	6	6	0	0	20	1	18
Guinea-Bissau	6	1	3	2	5	11	6
Guinea	6	0	4	2	5	11	4
Sudan	6	0	3	3	5	12	3
GROUP J							
Congo DR	6	3	2	1	9	3	11
Benin	6	3	1	2	5	4	10
Tanzania	6	2	2	2	6	8	8
Madagascar	6	1	1	4	4	9	4

THIRD ROUND

Egypt v. **Senegal**:	1-0, 0-1 (aet): agg. 1-1	
Senegal	3-1 on penalties	
Cameroon v. **Algeria**:	0-1, 2-1 (aet): agg. 2-2	
Cameroon	on away goals rule	
Ghana v. **Nigeria**:	0-0, 1-1: agg. 1-1	
Ghana	on away goals rule	

Congo DR v. **Morocco**:	1-1, 1-4	
Morocco	5-2 on agg.	
Mali v. **Tunisia**:	0-1, 0-0	
Tunisia	1-0 on agg.	

ASIA (AFC)

SECOND ROUND

Teams	P	W	D	D	GF	GA	Pts
GROUP A							
Syria	8	7	0	1	22	7	21
China PR	8	6	1	1	30	3	19
Philippines	8	3	2	3	12	11	11
Maldives	8	2	1	5	7	20	7
Guam	8	0	0	8	2	32	0
GROUP B							
Australia	8	8	0	0	28	2	24
Kuwait	8	4	2	2	19	7	14
Jordan	8	4	2	2	13	3	14
Nepal	8	2	0	6	4	22	6
Chinese Taipei	8	0	0	8	4	34	0
GROUP C							
IR Iran	8	6	0	2	34	4	18
Iraq	8	5	2	1	14	4	17
Bahrain	8	4	3	1	15	4	15
Hong Kong	8	1	2	5	4	13	5
Cambodia	8	0	1	7	2	44	1
GROUP D							
Saudi Arabia	8	6	2	0	22	4	20
Uzbekistan	8	5	0	3	18	9	15
Palestine	8	3	1	4	10	10	10
Singapore	8	2	1	5	7	22	7
Yemen	8	1	2	5	6	18	5
GROUP E							
*Qatar	8	7	1	0	18	1	22
Oman	8	6	0	2	16	6	18
India	8	1	4	3	6	7	7
Afghanistan	8	1	3	4	5	15	6
Bangladesh	8	0	2	6	3	19	2
GROUP F							
Japan	8	8	0	0	46	2	24
Tajikistan	8	4	1	3	14	12	13
Kyrgyzstan	8	3	1	4	19	12	10
Mongolia	8	2	0	6	3	27	6
Myanmar	8	2	0	6	6	35	6
GROUP G							
UAE	8	6	0	2	23	7	18
Vietnam	8	5	2	1	13	5	17
Malaysia	8	4	0	4	10	12	12
Thailand	8	2	3	3	9	9	9
Indonesia	8	0	1	7	5	27	1
GROUP H							
Korea Republic	6	5	1	0	22	1	16
Lebanon	6	3	1	2	11	8	10
Turkmenistan	6	3	0	3	8	11	9
Sri Lanka	6	0	0	6	2	23	0
Korea DPR withdrew							

Qatar competed because this stage also served as the qualifying competition for the AFC Asian Cup.

Withdrawal of Korea DPR meant results against fifth-placed teams of each group were not counted in ranking of group runners-up: hence China PR and Oman progressed to the third round with group winners (with the exception of FIFA World Cup hosts Qatar).

THIRD ROUND

GROUP A	P	W	D	D	GF	GA	Pts
IR Iran	10	8	1	1	15	4	25
Korea Rep.	10	7	2	1	13	3	23
UAE	10	3	3	4	7	7	12
Iraq	10	1	6	3	6	12	9
Syria	10	1	3	6	9	16	6
Lebanon	10	1	3	6	5	13	6

GROUP B	P	W	D	D	GF	GA	Pts
Saudi Arabia	10	7	2	1	12	6	23
Japan	10	7	1	2	12	4	22
Australia	10	4	3	3	15	9	15
Oman	10	4	2	4	11	10	14
China PR	10	1	3	6	9	19	6
Vietnam	10	1	1	8	8	19	4

ABOVE: IR Iran's Hossein Kanani and Samam Ghodoos celebrate reaching the finals after victory over Iraq in Tehran.

EUROPE (UEFA)

SECOND ROUND

Teams	P	W	D	D	GF	GA	Pts
GROUP A							
Serbia	8	6	2	0	18	9	20
Portugal	8	5	2	1	17	6	17
Rep. Ireland	8	2	3	3	11	8	9
Luxembourg	8	3	0	5	8	18	9
Azerbaijan	8	0	1	7	5	18	1
GROUP B							
Spain	8	6	1	1	15	5	19
Sweden	8	5	0	3	12	6	15
Greece	8	2	4	2	8	8	10
Georgia	8	2	1	5	6	12	7
Kosovo	8	1	2	5	5	15	5
GROUP C							
Switzerland	8	5	3	0	15	2	18
Italy	8	4	4	0	13	2	16
N. Ireland	8	2	3	3	6	7	9
Bulgaria	8	2	2	4	6	14	8
Lithuania	8	1	0	7	4	19	3
GROUP D							
France	8	5	3	0	18	3	18
Ukraine	8	2	6	0	11	8	12
Finland	8	3	2	3	10	10	11
Bosnia and H.	8	1	4	3	9	12	7
Kazakhstan	8	0	3	5	5	20	3
GROUP E							
Belgium	8	6	2	0	25	6	20
Wales	8	4	3	1	14	9	15
Czech Republic	8	4	2	2	14	9	14
Estonia	8	1	1	6	9	21	4
Belarus	8	1	0	7	7	24	3
GROUP F							
Denmark	10	9	0	1	30	3	27
Scotland	10	7	2	1	17	7	23
Israel	10	5	1	4	23	21	16
Austria	10	5	1	4	19	17	16
Faroe Islands	10	1	1	8	7	23	4
Moldova	10	0	1	9	5	30	1

Teams	P	W	D	D	GF	GA	Pts
GROUP G							
Netherlands	10	7	2	1	33	8	23
Turkey	10	6	3	1	27	16	21
Norway	10	5	3	2	15	8	18
Montenegro	10	3	3	4	14	15	12
Latvia	10	2	3	5	11	14	9
Gibraltar	10	0	0	10	4	43	0
GROUP H							
Croatia	10	7	2	1	21	4	23
Russia	10	7	1	2	19	6	22
Slovakia	10	3	5	2	17	10	14
Slovenia	10	4	2	4	13	12	14
Cyprus	10	1	2	7	4	21	5
Malta	10	1	2	7	9	30	5
GROUP I							
England	10	8	2	0	39	3	26
Poland	10	6	2	2	30	11	20
Albania	10	6	0	4	12	12	18
Hungary	10	5	2	3	19	13	17
Andorra	10	2	0	8	8	24	6
San Marino	10	0	0	10	1	46	0
GROUP J							
Germany	10	9	0	1	36	4	27
N. Macedonia	10	5	3	2	23	11	18
Romania	10	5	2	3	13	8	17
Armenia	10	3	3	4	9	20	12
Iceland	10	2	3	5	12	18	9
Liechtenstein	10	0	1	9	2	34	1

RIGHT: Portugal's Danilo Pereira and Pepe take on North Macedonia's Aleksandar Trajkovski in their play-off final.

NORTH, CENTRAL AMERICA and CARIBBEAN (Concacaf)

THIRD ROUND

Teams	P	W	D	D	GF	GA	Pts
Canada	14	8	4	2	23	7	28
Mexico	14	8	4	2	17	8	28
USA	14	7	4	3	21	10	25
Costa Rica	14	7	4	3	13	8	25
Panama	14	6	3	5	17	19	21
Jamaica	14	2	5	7	12	22	11
El Salvador	14	2	4	8	8	18	10
Honduras	14	0	4	10	7	26	4

SOUTH AMERICA (CONMEBOL)

THIRD ROUND

Teams	P	W	D	D	GF	GA	Pts
Brazil	17*	14	3	0	40	5	45
Argentina	17*	11	6	0	27	8	39
Uruguay	18	8	4	6	22	22	28
Ecuador	18	7	5	6	27	19	26
Peru	18	7	3	8	19	22	24
Colombia	18	5	8	5	20	19	23
Chile	18	5	4	9	19	26	19
Paraguay	18	3	7	8	12	26	16
Bolivia	18	4	3	11	23	42	15
Venezuela	18	3	1	14	14	34	10

Brazil v. Argentina tie rearranged

OCEANIA (OFC)

GROUP STAGE

Teams	P	W	D	D	GF	GA	Pts
GROUP A							
Solomon Is.	1	1	0	0	3	1	3
Tahiti	1	0	0	1	1	3	0

Vanuatu withdrew
Cook Islands withdrew

Teams	P	W	D	D	GF	GA	Pts
GROUP B							
New Zealand	3	3	0	0	12	1	9
Papua NG	3	2	0	1	3	2	6
Fiji	3	1	0	2	3	7	3
N. Caledonia	3	0	0	3	2	10	0

FINAL STAGE

Semi-finals:
Solomon Islands v. **Papua New Guinea**: 3-2
New Zealand v. Tahiti: 1-0

Final:
Solomon Islands v. **New Zealand** 0-5

RIGHT: Brazil's Matheus Cunha escapes Argentina's Cristian Romero during their 0–0 draw in San Juan.

THE FINAL DRAW

The last and most important countdown to the finals of the FIFA World Cup 2022 Qatar was celebrated by the final draw staged at the Doha Exhibition and Convention Center on 1 April.

The draw yielded eight well-balanced groups, with highlights including former champions Spain and Germany being placed together in Group E, hosts Qatar being handed a debut assignment against Ecuador, and a blockbuster opening-day match between the Netherlands and Senegal.

The draw, watched eagerly by fans all around the world, lasted a little more than an hour. FIFA president Gianni Infantino welcomed the world with an appeal for peace. Introductions were delivered by actor Idris Elba and sports broadcaster Reshmin Chowdhury, while France coach Didier Deschamps brought on stage the trophy he had won as captain in 1998 and then national-team supremo in 2018.

Veteran favourites from around the world had been drafted in to fill up the slots in the awaiting match schedule. The draw was conducted by the ex-England midfielder Jermaine Jenas, with former US Women's World Cup winner Carli Lloyd and British-Jamaican sports presenter Samantha Johnson. Breaking open the all-important caskets with country names and match identities was another star team led by former World Cup winners Cafu and Lothar Matthäus from Brazil and Germany respectively.

Other assistants included Nigeria's Jay-Jay Okocha, Australia's Tim Cahill, Qatar's Adel Ahmed Malalla, IR Iran's Ali Daei, Algeria's Rabah Madjer and Bora Milutinović, the only coach to have managed at five consecutive editions of the FIFA World Cup with different teams: Mexico (1986), Costa Rica (1990), USA (1994), Nigeria (1998) and China PR (2002).

Malalla said: "I'm thrilled to have been a draw assistant in my home country, and proud of Qatar. A FIFA World Cup in our region is a dream come true for every Arab footballer and football fan. This generation will make history on the pitch and we cannot wait to welcome the world here in just a few months' time."

The key statistics governing the draw were the most recent FIFA/Coca-Cola World Ranking, whose latest computation had seen Brazil take over the number one spot from the long-time leaders Belgium. This guided the allocation of teams. Pot 1 comprised Qatar as hosts and the seven highest-ranked qualified teams; Pot 2 had the next eight highest-ranked qualified teams; Pot 3 the eight highest-qualified after that, and Pot 4 the five best-ranked teams.

Also factored in were the two winners of the scheduled intercontinental play-offs, plus one from the European play-offs. Teams from the same confederation were kept apart in the groups, with the exception of Europe, which was permitted a maximum of two countries per group. Jenas and his colleagues then set the balls rolling towards the ultimate outcomes

LEFT: Brazil hero Cafu picks out hosts Qatar at the World Cup draw.

ABOVE: All attention is on the stage for the draw at the Doha Exhibition and Convention Center.

being decided in Qatar in November and December.

The occasion of the final draw is not only a matching of dates, teams and stadiums – essential as is all of this. The draw also provides a stage around which other essential features of the FIFA World Cup finals are introduced, such as the matchball, the mascot and the music.

Al Rihla – "the journey" in Arabic – has been designed and produced by adidas as the Official Match Ball. This is the 14th successive World Cup ball that the company has created and, according to a promotional statement, it "travels faster in flight than any ball in the tournament's history." Jean-François Pathy, FIFA's marketing

director, described it as "a stunning, sustainable and high-quality ball that will be enjoyed by stars performing at the top of their game on the world's biggest stage in Qatar, as well as grassroots players everywhere".

The ball was designed with sustainability as a priority. Al Rihla is the first FIFA World Cup ball to be made exclusively with water-based inks and glues.

The Official Mascot for the FIFA World Cup 2022 Qatar is La'eeb. This is an Arabic word meaning a super-skilled player, and the mascot, which will become familiar to fans around the world, was also unveiled during the final draw. Khalid Ali Al Mawlawi, from

the Supreme Committee for Delivery & Legacy, said: "We are delighted to unveil La'eeb as the Official Mascot for the first FIFA World Cup in the Middle East and Arab world. He belongs to a parallel mascot-verse that is indescribable. We encourage everyone to imagine what it looks like."

Then, of course, no FIFA World Cup would be complete without its own music. Also launched on the eve of the draw was the Official Soundtrack, which kicked off with the release of the single *Hayya Hayya* (*Better Together*), featuring Trinidad Cardona, Davido and Aisha.

The football world will be both listening and watching all the way to the final on 18 December.

FIFA WORLD CUP
Qatar2022

· · · · · ❖ · · · · ·

MEET THE
TEAMS

Football fans around the planet will unite in focusing their attention on Qatar once the FIFA World Cup kicks off on 21 November at the Al Bayt Stadium in Al Khor. A magnetic sporting attraction will be provided by 32 teams, who criss-crossed their respective continents to earn their place at the first World Cup in the Middle East. Traditional favourites with title-winning ambitions, including all four semi-finalists from Russia in 2018, await challengers old and new.

· · · · · ❖ · · · · ·

QATAR

Qatar are the first hosts since Uruguay at the inaugural FIFA World Cup in 1930 not to have previously appeared at the tournament. But while the country is small in size, it is large in ambition and thorough in its preparation.

COACH
FÉLIX SÁNCHEZ

Félix Sánchez will celebrate his 47th birthday during this World Cup, having been born in Barcelona on 13 December 1975. Sánchez is unusual among his colleagues at the tournament in not possessing a notable playing record. Instead, he focused on a coaching career launched in the youth sections at Barcelona. The quality of his work led to an appointment at the Aspire Academy in 2006. In 2013, he was appointed coach of the Qatar U-19s, whom he led to the AFC title a year later. He succeeded Jorge Fossati in charge of the senior team in 2017. Two years later, his team won the AFC Asian Cup for the first time.

The modern state of Qatar began life as a British protectorate in 1916. Oil was discovered in the 1930s, which prompted advances in all spheres of society and led to independence in September 1971. British oil workers had brought football to the Gulf in the 1940s and 1950s and the Qatar Football Association was founded in 1960. Membership of the worldwide FIFA family was attained in 1970, when the national team made their debut against neighbouring Bahrain.

Qatar contested the qualifying competition for every World Cup between 1978 and 2018, albeit without success. However, their ambition to rise up the international ladder has never been in doubt. Football has featured high among the stream of sporting championships that Qatar has hosted. A notable first was the FIFA U-20 World Cup in 1995, when Qatar stepped in to play host at short notice. The country has also staged the FIFA Club World Cup twice in addition to the AFC Asian Cup on two occasions and, most recently, the inaugural FIFA Arab Cup™ in 2021.

Milestones have been achieved on and off the pitch. In 1981, Qatar were runners-up at the U-20 World Cup in Australia, beating both Brazil and England on their way to a final defeat by West Germany. The Qataris made their debut in the men's football tournament at the 1984 Olympic Games in Los Angeles, before progressing to the quarter-finals in Barcelona in 1992. Even better was to come later that year, as star striker Mubarak Mustafa led them to a first Arabian Gulf Cup triumph in Doha. Qatar finished two points clear of Bahrain, Saudi Arabia and the United Arab Emirates.

ABOVE: Qatar's national team, pride of the host nation.

⬢ ONES TO WATCH

ALMOEZ ALI
BORN: 19 AUGUST 1996
CLUB: AL-DUHAIL (QAT)

Almoez Ali, the captain of Qatar Stars League club Al Duhail, set an AFC Asian Cup record when he scored nine goals to fire Qatar to success in 2019. Ali was born in Sudan and moved to Qatar as a child. He started at the Al-Mesaimeer club at the age of seven and then progressed to the Aspire Academy and Lekhwiya. From 2014 to 2016, he had spells in Europe with Eupen (Belgium), LASK (Austria) and lower-league Cultural y Deportiva Leonesa (Spain). Ali then returned to Lekhwiya and, after the club's merger with El-Jaish, led the newly renamed Al-Duhail to the league title.

HASSAN AL-HAYDOS
BORN: 11 DECEMBER 1990
CLUB: AL SADD (QAT)

Hassan Al-Haydos has enjoyed a 12-year international career that has established him as Qatar's record international, with more than 140 appearances, and as one of the country's most successful marksmen. Al-Haydos, born in Doha, has spent his entire career with Al Sadd, whom he joined at the age of eight. He made his senior debut for Qatar at 17 in a 2010 FIFA World Cup™ qualifier against Bahrain and was still only 20 when his goals lifted Al Sadd to the AFC Champions League crown, which they backed up with a third-place finish at the FIFA Club World Cup 2011.

RECORD AT PREVIOUS TOURNAMENTS

1930	DID NOT EXIST
1934	DID NOT EXIST
1938	DID NOT EXIST
1950	DID NOT EXIST
1954	DID NOT EXIST
1958	DID NOT EXIST
1962	DID NOT EXIST
1966	DID NOT EXIST
1970	DID NOT EXIST
1974	WITHDREW
1978	DID NOT QUALIFY
1982	DID NOT QUALIFY
1986	DID NOT QUALIFY
1990	DID NOT QUALIFY
1994	DID NOT QUALIFY
1998	DID NOT QUALIFY
2002	DID NOT QUALIFY
2006	DID NOT QUALIFY
2010	DID NOT QUALIFY
2014	DID NOT QUALIFY
2018	DID NOT QUALIFY

More success was inevitable. Qatar won the football gold medal as hosts at the 2006 Asian Games in between carrying off the Arabian Gulf Cup in 2004 and again in Saudi Arabia in 2014. By that time, significant international attention had been attracted by the World Cup award. This newly acquired status put the national team under extra pressure. They responded in style by winning the aforementioned Gulf title in 2014 and then their first major international prize at the AFC Asian Cup in 2019.

Qatar, now coached by Félix Sánchez and reducing their earlier reliance on naturalised players, won all their seven games, overcoming Japan 3-1 in the final. Striker Almoez Ali set his side on their way in the showpiece by scoring his ninth goal of the competition – a new record – with a spectacular overhead kick. The other goals were added by Abdulaziz Hatem and Akram Afif.

Further international experience followed at the CONMEBOL *Copa América* and last year's Concacaf Gulf Cup, where Qatar reached the semi-finals before losing 1-0 to the USA. A busy 2021 campaign also saw Qatar competing in the AFC Asian Cup qualifying competition, undertaking a series of European friendlies and then finishing third as hosts in the Arab Cup.

Sánchez's 23-man Arab Cup squad featured ten players with more than 50 international appearances. These included goalkeeper Saad al Sheeb, defenders Ró-Ró, Abdelkarim Hassan, Tarek Salman and Boualem Khoukhi, midfielders Abdulaziz Hatem and Karim Boudiaf, and forward Hassan Al-Haydos, plus AFC Asian Cup heroes Ali and Afif. All the squad were drawn from local clubs, including half from Al Sadd, the record 15-time champions of the Qatar Stars League.

ECUADOR

Ecuador are appearing at the FIFA World Cup finals for the fourth time. Their ambition is to emulate their achievement in 2006. In Germany, *La Tri* – or *Tricolor* – marked their debut by reaching the round of 16 before being eliminated after a 1-0 defeat to England.

COACH
GUSTAVO ALFARO

Gustavo Alfaro, born on 14 August 1962, in Argentina, has been the national coach of Ecuador since succeeding Jordi Cruyff in August 2020. Alfaro played league football at a modest level in Argentina before retiring in 1992 to develop a successful career as a coach. He led Quilmes into the CONMEBOL *Libertadores* and had a short spell with San Lorenzo before guiding Arsenal de Sarandi to success in the 2012 *Clausura* championship and then the *Copa Sudamericana*. Later, he worked in Saudi Arabia with Al-Ahli of Jeddah before returning home to successive posts with Arsenal de Sarandi again, Tigre, Gimnasia y Esgrima, Huracán and Boca Juniors.

Captain of Ecuador in 2006 was central defender Iván Hurtado, one of the greatest footballers in the country's history. He made a South American record 168 international appearances for Ecuador between 1992 and 2014 and, after retiring, was elected to the national assembly.

Ranking alongside Hurtado among Ecuador's greatest players was striker Pedro Alberto Spencer. He won South America's prestigious CONMEBOL *Libertadores* club championship three times in the 1960s with Peñarol of Uruguay and still holds the competition record of 54 goals between 1960 and 1972.

Ecuador's realistic qualifying challenge this time around in South America's extensive liguilla had been to chase down the fourth certain place behind perpetual favourites Brazil, Argentina and Uruguay. The schedule was delayed and disrupted by worldwide pandemic restrictions on travel. Eventually, Ecuador made a losing start away to Argentina, but coach Gustavo Alfaro said he was encouraged that the difference between the teams was only an early penalty converted by Leo Messi.

The pandemic restrictions also meant that no fans were present in Quito to enjoy Ecuador's follow-up success by 4-2 at home to Uruguay in their second match. The DC United forward Michael Estrada scored two of the goals.

A late penalty from Carlos Gruezo secured a 3-2 victory at altitude against Bolivia in La Paz and then Estrada was again on target in an outstanding 6-1 victory over Colombia. Defeats in Brazil and at home to Peru then stalled Ecuador's momentum and led to a run of four games without a

ABOVE: Ecuador, back at the finals at last.

⬢ ONES TO WATCH

ENNER VALENCIA
BORN: 4 NOVEMBER 1989
CLUB: FENERBAHCE (TUR)

Enner Valencia is captain of Ecuador and record marksman with nearly 40 goals in more than 70 appearances since his debut in 2012. He is Ecuador's joint top scorer at the World Cup finals after scoring three times in Brazil in 2014. Valencia was born and brought up in Esmeraldas and built a teenage reputation with Emelec.
In 2013 he led Emelec to success in the championship and was top scorer in the *Copa Sudamericana*. These achievements prompted transfers abroad to Pachuca and Tigres in Mexico, England's West Ham and Everton, then Turkey's Fenerbahce in 2020.

MICHAEL ESTRADA
BORN: 7 APRIL 1996
CLUB: D.C. UNITED (USA)

Michael Estrada was Ecuador's six-goal leading scorer in the South American qualifying section for the FIFA World Cup finals. He was born in Guayaquil, began with Macara of Ambato and maintained a goalscoring reputation with El Nacional and Independiente del Valle. Estrada moved to Tolima in Mexico in 2019 and was then loaned this year to D.C. United. He made his senior national-team debut in 2017 and his goals against Uruguay, Colombia, Paraguay, Bolivia and Peru were crucial in Ecuador's success in qualifying for the World Cup finals.

RECORD AT PREVIOUS TOURNAMENTS

1930	DID NOT ENTER
1934	DID NOT ENTER
1938	DID NOT ENTER
1950	WITHDREW
1954	DID NOT ENTER
1958	DID NOT QUALIFY
1962	DID NOT QUALIFY
1966	DID NOT QUALIFY
1970	DID NOT QUALIFY
1974	DID NOT QUALIFY
1978	DID NOT QUALIFY
1982	DID NOT QUALIFY
1986	DID NOT QUALIFY
1990	DID NOT QUALIFY
1994	DID NOT QUALIFY
1998	DID NOT QUALIFY
2002	FIRST ROUND
2006	ROUND OF 16
2010	DID NOT QUALIFY
2014	FIRST ROUND
2018	DID NOT QUALIFY

win before results turned for the better with a 3-0 home win over Bolivia.

A mixed set of results in the run-in eventually saw Ecuador cross the qualifying line despite a 3-1 defeat by Paraguay in the penultimate matchday. Heroes of the campaign included the captain Enner Valencia and forward Estrada who was the team's six-goal top scorer.

Football had been brought to Ecuador in the late 19th century by the brothers Juan Alfredo and Roberto Wright. They founded the first recorded club, Guayaquil, and the game's popularity led to the creation

of the Ecuadorian Football Association in 1925. Five years later, Ecuador were offered the opportunity to compete at the inaugural World Cup finals in Uruguay, but declined.

Only after achieving a fourth-place finish at a South American championship tournament in 1959 was the association persuaded to enter the World Cup for the first time. They failed to qualify in 11 successive attempts before finally reaching the group stage in Japan and Korea Republic in 2002. Since then, Ecuador have missed out on the World Cup finals only in 2010 and 2018.

Record 16-time champions Barcelona of Guayaquil have been Ecuador's most successful club on the international stage. They twice finished runners-up in the CONMEBOL *Libertadores*, in 1990 and 1998. One of the stars of their team in 1998 was forward Augustín Delgado, who had the honour in 2002 of scoring Ecuador's first-ever goal at the World Cup finals, against Mexico. Delgado, who also played his club football in Mexico and England, held the national-team record of 31 goals in 71 appearances before being overtaken by current captain Enner Valencia.

GROUP A

SENEGAL

FIFA WORLD CUP Qatar2022

Senegal want to build on their status as African champions and emulate their best-ever run to the quarter-finals of 2002 in Japan and Korea Republic. Star forward Sadio Mané and his team-mates have already proved their ability to withstand high-level pressure.

COACH
ALIOU CISSÉ

Aliou Cissé, born on 24 March 1976, is one of the longest-serving national-team coaches in African football history. Cissé, on his appointment in 2015, already possessed FIFA World Cup pedigree as the player who had captained Senegal to the quarter-finals in 2002. He was then the interim manager in 2012 and coached the Olympic team. He guided Senegal to the final of the Africa Cup of Nations in 2019 and ultimate success early this year. Previously, his playing career had taken him to French clubs Lille, Sedan, Paris Saint-Germain, Montpellier and Nîmes, plus England's Birmingham City and Portsmouth.

The first test was the Africa Cup of Nations in Cameroon. Senegal won their first-round group but without being at their best. They started with a narrow win over Zimbabwe, courtesy of a late Mané penalty. Then they drew 0-0 with both Guinea and Malawi to progress to the knockout stage, where victories over Cabo Verde, Equatorial Guinea and Burkina Faso took them to the final against holders Egypt. Senegal forced a goalless draw with the seven-time champions before winning 4-2 on penalties.

That was February. By then Senegal and Egypt knew they would be facing each other once more, this time home and away, with a place in the World Cup finals at stake.

Senegal had reached the final round of qualifying by winning a second round mini-league in the autumn of 2021. They were unbeaten in all six games and finished eight points clear of runners-up Togo in Group H. Mané and Ismaïla Sarr both scored three times.

The draw for the third round, which matched them with Egypt – and Mané's Liverpool club-mate Mohamed Salah – was then undertaken during the Africa Cup of Nations finals. On 25 March, Senegal lost 1-0 to Egypt in front of a 65,000 crowd at the Cairo International Stadium. Four days later, in Dakar, a third-minute goal from Villarreal's Boulaye Dia squared the aggregate. Neither side managed a goal in the rest of the 90 minutes or extra time, so it all came down to penalties once more.

Both teams missed their opening two kicks and then successful conversions from Sarr and Bamba Dieng put Senegal 2-1 ahead. Mané scored from the fifth kick to condemn

ABOVE: Senegal reached the 2022 finals via a shoot-out.

❋ ONES TO WATCH

EDOUARD MENDY
BORN: 1 MARCH 1992
CLUB: CHELSEA (ENG)

Edouard Mendy could have qualified to play for Guinea-Bissau and France as well as Senegal. He has enjoyed a remarkable year. Mendy starred in shoot-out victories over Egypt in the Africa Cup of Nations and in the FIFA World Cup qualifiers. In between, he won the FIFA Club World Cup with Chelsea. He joined English Premier League Chelsea for EUR 30m in 2020. In his first season, he equalled the record of nine clean sheets in the victorious UEFA Champions League campaign. He was subsequently hailed by FIFA as The Best Goalkeeper of the Year.

CHEIKHOU KOUYATÉ
BORN: 21 DECEMBER 1989
CLUB: CRYSTAL PALACE (ENG)

Cheikhou Kouyaté, with more than 80 appearances for Senegal, has been compared with former France anchor Patrick Vieira. He made his senior national-team debut in 2012 after starring at youth and Olympic level. Kouyaté's club career took him from Belgium's Anderlecht in 2014 to English Premier League club West Ham United and then on to London rivals Crystal Palace in 2018. He made his Senegal debut in 2012 and helped them reach the quarter-finals of the Olympic finals in London. He was a key member of the team that won the Africa Cup of Nations in February.

RECORD AT PREVIOUS TOURNAMENTS

1930	DID NOT EXIST
1934	DID NOT EXIST
1938	DID NOT EXIST
1950	DID NOT EXIST
1954	DID NOT EXIST
1958	DID NOT EXIST
1962	DID NOT ENTER
1966	WITHDREW
1970	DID NOT QUALIFY
1974	DID NOT QUALIFY
1978	DID NOT QUALIFY
1982	DID NOT QUALIFY
1986	DID NOT QUALIFY
1990	DID NOT QUALIFY
1994	DID NOT QUALIFY
1998	DID NOT QUALIFY
2002	QUARTER-FINALS
2006	DID NOT QUALIFY
2010	DID NOT QUALIFY
2014	DID NOT QUALIFY
2018	FIRST ROUND

Egypt to another shoot-out defeat and send Senegal to Qatar. Mané was magnanimous in victory. He said: "I won twice and he (Salah) lost twice. I was luckier to come out on top. But I am very proud that we won the Africa Cup and qualified for the World Cup. It's a dream I always had."

Senegal, founded in 1958, had been one of the first newly independent countries from former French West Africa to qualify for the finals of the Africa Cup of Nations in 1965. They finished fourth, were fourth again in 1990, quarter-finalists as hosts in 1992 and runners-up in 2002. In the final in the Malian capital of Bamako, they lost 3-2 on penalties to Cameroon after a goalless draw.

That same team then progressed to the FIFA World Cup finals for the first time. Stars such as winger El Hadji Diouf and goalkeeper Tony Sylva not only shared the honour of competing in the opening match but made it memorable by defeating champions France 1-0 in Seoul. Papa Bouba Diop scored the most famous goal in Senegalese history.

Senegal proved this was no fluke by drawing 1-1 and 3-3 with Denmark and Uruguay respectively to advance to the round of 16. Coach Bruno Metsu's men then defeated Sweden 2-1 before losing 1-0 on an extra-time golden goal to Turkey in Osaka.

Momentum has been maintained at continental level with mostly continuing participation in the finals of the Africa Cup of Nations. But a return to the FIFA World Cup eluded them until 2018. They were grouped with Colombia, Japan and Poland. Colombia won the group, Japan and Senegal finished level on points, goal difference and goals scored, but Senegal became the first team ever eliminated on an inferior fair-play assessment.

NETHERLANDS

FIFA WORLD CUP
Qatar2022™

The FIFA World Cup is a natural stage for the Dutch national team. The Netherlands have been runners-up on three occasions and finished third in 2014. They have reclaimed a place at the top table after having been surprising absentees from Russia in 2018.

COACH
LOUIS VAN GAAL

Louis van Gaal, born on 8 August 1951, is in his third stint as Dutch national-team coach. The former Royal Antwerp, Telstar, Sparta Rotterdam and AZ Alkmaar midfielder missed out on World Cup qualification in 2002, led the Netherlands to third place in Brazil in 2014 and returned to the helm in July 2021. Van Gaal also boasts a stellar club coaching CV, with tenures at Ajax, Barcelona, AZ Alkmaar, Bayern Munich and Manchester United. He has won more than 20 major trophies, including the UEFA Champions League, league and cup titles in the Netherlands, Spain and Germany, and the FA Cup in England.

Van Gaal took charge of the national team for the third time after UEFA EURO 2020, getting the nod to replace Frank de Boer following the country's round-of-16 exit. The squad Van Gaal inherited included outstanding players such as midfielder Georginio Wijnaldum and free-scoring striker Memphis Depay, as well as Virgil van Dijk.

The Netherlands had been drawn in a testing World Cup qualifying group, with Turkey and Norway their most dangerous rivals. Turkey underlined their credentials by defeating the Dutch 4-2 at the Atatürk Olympic Stadium in Istanbul in the opening round of matches in March 2021. The Dutch proved their fighting spirit by recovering from 3-0 down to just 3-2 before conceding a fourth as they pressed for an equaliser in the closing stages.

Victories at home to Latvia and away to Gibraltar provided the platform on which to build when qualifying resumed in September last year. Turkey were the early group leaders, with the Netherlands and Norway both a point adrift after a 1-1 draw in Oslo. *Oranje* then leapfrogged the Turks after beating them 6-1 in Amsterdam. Depay scored a hat-trick, including a penalty. He subsequently bagged braces in the 6-0 victory over Gibraltar and the 2-2 draw in Montenegro.

Those goals set up a last-matchday showdown. The Netherlands had 20 points, with Turkey and opponents Norway both on 18. The Dutch needed to avoid defeat to reach Qatar but went one better by winning 2-0 through goals from Steven Bergwijn and then Depay in stoppage time. The Barcelona striker ended as the group's top marksman with 12 goals. The

ABOVE: Netherlands have been runners-up on three occasions.

⬢ ONES TO WATCH

MEMPHIS DEPAY
BORN: 13 FEBRUARY 1994
CLUB: BARCELONA (SPA)

With 12 goals, Memphis Depay was the joint-top scorer in the European qualifying section for the World Cup. He made his senior debut in 2013, and has since scored at a rate of roughly a goal every two caps. Depay made his name at PSV Eindhoven, whom he fired to the league title in 2014-2015 as the division's leading marksman. His 22 goals also saw him win the Johan Cruyff Trophy for the *Eredivisie*'s most promising young player of the year. Depay then transferred to Manchester United before moving on to Lyon, then Barcelona, following UEFA EURO 2020.

GEORGINIO WIJNALDUM
BORN: 11 NOVEMBER 1990
CLUB: PARIS SAINT-GERMAIN (FRA)

Georginio Wijnaldum was only 16 when he became the youngest player to feature for Feyenoord in 2007, before moving to PSV Eindhoven, making his senior national-team debut and being voted the Dutch Footballer of the Year. He spent one season with Newcastle United before transferring to Liverpool, with whom he won the UEFA Champions League in 2019 and then the UEFA Super Cup, FIFA Club World Cup and Premier League. Wijnaldum signed for Paris Saint-Germain in 2021.

RECORD AT PREVIOUS TOURNAMENTS

1930	DID NOT ENTER
1934	FIRST ROUND
1938	FIRST ROUND
1950	DID NOT ENTER
1954	DID NOT ENTER
1958	DID NOT QUALIFY
1962	DID NOT QUALIFY
1966	DID NOT QUALIFY
1970	DID NOT QUALIFY
1974	RUNNERS-UP
1978	RUNNERS-UP
1982	DID NOT QUALIFY
1986	DID NOT QUALIFY
1990	SECOND ROUND
1994	QUARTER-FINALS
1998	FOURTH PLACE
2002	DID NOT QUALIFY
2006	SECOND ROUND
2010	RUNNERS-UP
2014	THIRD PLACE
2018	DID NOT QUALIFY

Netherlands' reliance on his eye for an opening was underlined by the fact that their second-leading scorer was Davy Klaassen with four goals.

The Dutch were among Europe's leading amateur teams in the early 1900s. They reached the semi-finals of four consecutive editions of the Olympic Games from 1908 to 1924 and won the bronze medal twice. The modernisation of the domestic game in the mid-1950s brought the introduction of professionalism and success both at home and abroad for Ajax, Feyenoord and PSV Eindhoven.

In the late 1960s and early 1970s,

legendary coach Rinus Michels oversaw a "total football" revolution. Johan Cruyff inspired record champions Ajax to three successive triumphs in the European Cup (which is now the UEFA Champions League) between 1971 and 1973. A year later, the Dutch brought their stylish, all-action football to the World Cup in West Germany. A team also featuring playmaker Wim van Hanegem, energetic midfielder Johan Neeskens and raiding full-back Ruud Krol finished runners-up to their hosts. Four years later, the Dutch lost out to the host nation again, this time falling to Argentina in Buenos Aires.

The next generation also hit the headlines. Ruud Gullit, Marco van Basten, Frank Rijkaard and Ronald Koeman led the national team to victory at the UEFA EURO in 1988 in West Germany. Michels, the boss in 1974, was back as the coach. Success was achieved by defeating the Soviet Union 2-0 in the final in Munich. Captain Gullit scored the first goal and Van Basten volleyed a memorable second.

The Netherlands were semi-finalists at the 1998 FIFA World Cup™ and then runners-up for a third time in South Africa in 2010. On that occasion, they lost 1-0 to Spain in extra time.

ENGLAND

England have continued to improve ever since Gareth Southgate took over as manager. They are still in pursuit of a second major trophy after their success when hosting the 1966 FIFA World Cup™. Fourth place in 2018 was proof of progress.

COACH
GARETH SOUTHGATE

Southgate, born on 3 September 1970, has earned popularity and respect far beyond football for the way in which he has led England ever since he was promoted to the manager's role one match into the Russia 2018 qualifying campaign, from which he emerged with top marks. The former defender played 57 times for England between 1995 and 2004, including at UEFA EURO 1996 and France 1998. At club level, he played for Crystal Palace, Aston Villa and Middlesbrough, a team he also managed. Southgate then joined The FA and managed the U-21 team before taking up the senior role.

Russia 2018 saw England reach the FIFA World Cup semi-finals for the third time, following 1966 and 1990. Captain Harry Kane was the six-goal leading scorer and he and his team-mates then finished third in the UEFA Nations League in 2019. This was their springboard for the drama of UEFA EURO 2020. Wembley was the stage on which England finished runners-up to Italy in a penalty shoot-out after the match had finished 1-1 at the end of extra time.

England were always in command of European qualifying Group I from the opening 5-0 victory over San Marino in March 2021. Kane reopened his World Cup account in a 2-0 victory away to Albania and followed up with a penalty in a 2-1 defeat of Poland. The Poles had always been considered England's most dangerous group rivals and were defeated only by a late goal from Manchester United's Harry Maguire.

Southgate's men then turned their attention to the postponed UEFA EURO 2020 before resuming their winning World Cup ways in September with a 4-0 victory over Hungary, with Kane and Maguire on the scoresheet once again. A repeat victory over Albania was followed by a 1-1 draw with Poland in Warsaw, when England's 100 per cent record was spoilt by a stoppage-time strike from Damian Szymański.

Victory away to Andorra, a draw at home to Hungary and a 5-0 home win over Albania set England up to secure their place in Qatar with a 10-0 victory against San Marino in Serravalle. Kane scored three against Albania and four against San Marino, becoming one of only four England players ever to score hat-tricks in successive matches – and the first since 1957. England finished the group undefeated, six points clear of Poland, with 39 goals scored and only three conceded. No other

ABOVE: England reached the semi-finals in 2018 in Russia.

✦ ONES TO WATCH

JORDAN PICKFORD
BORN: 7 MARCH 1994
CLUB: EVERTON

Pickford has been England's first-choice goalkeeper since 2018 and the Russia World Cup campaign. His career began at Sunderland and he had six loan spells in the lower divisions before joining Everton for an initial transfer fee of GBP 25m in June 2017. His rise to international stardom was then meteoric. Pickford has represented England at U-16, U-17, U-18, U-19, U-20 and U-21 levels. He made his senior debut in November 2017 in a friendly against Germany and built a reputation as a penalty shoot-out hero at both Russia 2018 and the UEFA Nations League 2019 finals.

RAHEEM STERLING
BORN: 8 DECEMBER 1994
CLUB: MANCHESTER CITY

Raheem Sterling's career has taken him from the Queens Park Rangers academy to Manchester City, signing for what was then a record transfer fee for an English player of GBP 49m in 2015. He has scored well over 100 goals in the Premier League and has helped City to achieve repeated success in that competition, as well as the FA Cup and the EFL Cup. With England, Sterling progressed through all age-group levels to become a fixture of the side at the 2014 and 2018 FIFA World Cups and UEFA EURO 2016 and 2020.

RECORD AT PREVIOUS TOURNAMENTS

1930	DID NOT ENTER
1934	DID NOT ENTER
1938	DID NOT ENTER
1950	FIRST ROUND
1954	QUARTER-FINALS
1958	FIRST ROUND
1962	QUARTER-FINALS
1966	CHAMPIONS
1970	QUARTER-FINALS
1974	DID NOT QUALIFY
1978	DID NOT QUALIFY
1982	SECOND GROUP STAGE
1986	QUARTER-FINALS
1990	FOURTH PLACE
1994	DID NOT QUALIFY
1998	ROUND OF 16
2002	QUARTER-FINALS
2006	QUARTER-FINALS
2010	ROUND OF 16
2014	FIRST ROUND
2018	FOURTH PLACE

European team could match their goal difference of +36.

The experience gained in 2018 by goalkeeper Jordan Pickford, central defender Maguire, and forwards Raheem Sterling and Kane had now been supplemented by the emergence of Declan Rice in midfield, plus Phil Foden and Bukayo Saka in attack. With 12 goals, Kane was the overall joint leading scorer in European qualifying, together with the Netherlands' Memphis Depay.

This is England's seventh successive appearance at the final tournament and their 16th overall, befitting of their

place in the history of the game. The game's first governing body, The Football Association, was founded in 1863 and nine years later, England played in the very first international match against Scotland.

The FA joined FIFA in 1906, two years after its formation, though political disagreements led to England's absence from the World Cup in the 1930s. They were joint favourites on their finals debut in Brazil in 1950, but failed to progress beyond the first round.

Quarter-finals progress followed in 1954 and 1962 before England won the World Cup as hosts with a 4-2 extra-time

victory over West Germany at Wembley in 1966. Geoff Hurst made history as the only man to score a hat-trick in a World Cup final. His team-mates and fellow England legends included Bobby Charlton and captain Bobby Moore. The World Cup defence ended at the quarter-finals stage in Mexico four years later.

England's best subsequent tournament performances came when they reached the semi-finals in 1990 and 2018. In 1990, England lost on penalties to West Germany in Italy and in 2018, they lost 2-1 to Croatia after extra time.

IR IRAN

Qatar 2022 will be IR Iran's third consecutive appearance at the FIFA World Cup, and sixth in all. They are still waiting, however, to reach the knockout stage, but buoyed by a formidable qualifying campaign, they are hopeful of breaking new ground.

COACH
DRAGAN SKOČIĆ

Dragan Skočić, born on 3 September 1968, was appointed to replace Belgian Marc Wilmots midway through the second round of the Asian qualifying competition en route to Qatar. Skočić, who hails from Rijeka in Croatia, had spent a decade in the dugout with clubs in the Middle East, including stints with Al-Arabi (Kuwait), Al-Nassr (Saudi Arabia) and Iranian outfits Malavan, Foolad, Rayka Babol and Sanat Naft Abadan. This experience made him a fitting choice to pick up the reins with the campaign under way. Earlier in his coaching career, Skočić oversaw domestic cup success in Croatia with Rijeka and in Slovenia with Interblock.

The draw for the Asian qualifying competition had been staged at the AFC headquarters in Kuala Lumpur in pre-pandemic days back on 17 April 2019, with the fixture schedule also part of the qualifying process for the 2023 AFC Asian Cup. *Team Melli* were one of the beneficiaries of a bye courtesy of their position in the FIFA/Coca-Cola Men's World Ranking. They kicked off their campaign in the second round, in Group C, along with 2007 Asian champions Iraq, as well as Bahrain, Hong Kong and Cambodia.

IR Iran made a positive start in September 2019 with a 2-0 win in Hong Kong thanks to a goal in each half from Sardar Azmoun and Karim Ansarifard. The former scored a hat-trick and the latter bagged four goals the next time round, the following month, in a 14-0 drubbing of Cambodia at the Azadi Stadium in Tehran.

Next came a double setback in the shape of defeats in Bahrain and Iraq, but the Iranians subsequently won all their remaining games to top the group, finishing one point clear of Iraq.

They also boasted an impressive record of 34 goals scored and only four conceded. Ansarifard and Azmoun were the group's leading marksmen with seven goals apiece.

IR Iran and Iraq were drawn together again in the all-important third round, this time in Group A, together with challenging opposition from Korea Republic, the United Arab Emirates, Lebanon and Syria.

The COVID-19 pandemic forced the postponement of the opening matches by a full year from September 2020 to September 2021. A schedule set to stretch over 13 months was ultimately squeezed into six months. IR Iran, unperturbed, cruised through

ABOVE: IR Iran want to go beyond the first round in Qatar.

⬣ ONES TO WATCH

KARIM ANSARIFARD
BORN: 3 APRIL 1990
CLUB: AEK ATHENS (GRE)

Ansarifard was the Iranian league's top scorer in the 2011-2012 season, with 21 goals, when he attracted initial offers from Europe. But he stayed in his homeland before eventually embarking on a European adventure with Osasuna, Olympiacos and Nottingham Forest. Ansarifard also has experience of the conditions in Qatar, having had a stint with Al-Sailiya before joining AEK Athens. He scored the winning goal against Iceland on his senior international debut in 2009 and converted a late penalty in the draw with Portugal at the 2018 World Cup.

ALIREZA JAHANBAKHSH
BORN: 11 AUGUST 1993
CLUB: FEYENOORD (NET)

Alireza Jahanbakhsh played for IR Iran at U-20 and U-23 levels before featuring for the senior team at the World Cup in 2014 and 2018 as well as the AFC Asian Cup in 2015 and 2019. He moved to the Netherlands in 2013, joining NEC Nijmegen. He was subsequently snapped up by AZ Alkmaar, where his three-season spell was capped in 2017-2018, when he racked up 21 *Eredivisie* goals to become the first Asian top scorer in a major European league. He then spent three years with Brighton before returning to the Netherlands with Feyenoord.

RECORD AT PREVIOUS TOURNAMENTS

1930	DID NOT ENTER
1934	DID NOT ENTER
1938	DID NOT ENTER
1950	DID NOT ENTER
1954	DID NOT ENTER
1958	DID NOT ENTER
1962	DID NOT ENTER
1966	DID NOT ENTER
1970	DID NOT ENTER
1974	DID NOT QUALIFY
1978	FIRST ROUND
1982	WITHDREW
1986	DISQUALIFIED
1990	DID NOT QUALIFY
1994	DID NOT QUALIFY
1998	FIRST ROUND
2002	DID NOT QUALIFY
2006	FIRST ROUND
2010	DID NOT QUALIFY
2014	FIRST ROUND
2018	FIRST ROUND

their programme in style, and a 1-0 victory over Iraq in Tehran saw Dragan Skočić's team race ten points clear of the third-placed United Arab Emirates with three games to play and thus secure a flight to Qatar.

The decisive goal was scored by Porto striker Mehdi Taremi in the 48th minute. The pandemic-restricted crowd of 11,000 notably included around 2,000 women.

IR Iran emerged as a major Asian football power back in the 1960s. They won a hat-trick of Asian Cups starting in 1968, collected football gold at the 1974 Asian Games and qualified for

their first World Cup (the 1978 edition in Argentina). The highlight of their debut campaign in South America was holding Scotland to a 1-1 draw, but they finished bottom of their group.

It was not until almost two decades later that the country graced the tournament again, reaching the 1998 tournament in France. There, IR Iran achieved their first victory at the tournament by overcoming the USA 2-1 in Lyon. Nevertheless, a 2-0 defeat by Germany ended their campaign at the group stage.

IR Iran returned to the World Cup in 2006 but again failed to progress

beyond the first round, a tale repeated in Brazil in 2014 and Russia in 2018. The campaign in Russia saw *Team Melli* win only their second match at the competition, a 1-0 success against Morocco. Thanks to a draw with powerhouse Portugal, coach Carlos Queiroz's men finished third in their group with four points, the country's best-ever return.

A year later, IR Iran reached the semi-finals of the 2019 Asian Cup, after which Marc Wilmots led the country into the World Cup qualifiers before Skočić took over to clinch a berth in Qatar.

USA

The USA's first-round victory over England in 1950 remains one of the major upsets in the history of the FIFA World Cup. Team USA have reached seven of the past eight finals tournaments, and will jointly host the next celebration in 2026.

COACH
GREGG BERHALTER

Gregg Berhalter, born on 1 August 1973, played college soccer at the University of North Carolina and then moved to Europe in 1994 with Zwolle in the Netherlands. He later played in defence in England and Germany before winding down his career with Los Angeles Galaxy. Berhalter also played 44 times for the US between 1994 and 2006. He retired in 2011, was briefly assistant coach at Galaxy, then spent two years in charge of Sweden's Hammarby before returning home with Colombus Crew in 2013. He was appointed by U.S. Soccer in 2018 and should be the first person to both manage and play for the USA at a World Cup.

Qualifying for Qatar was no easy task. The USA had been surprising absentees from the finals in 2018. However, they were among the quintet of Concacaf nations whose position in the FIFA/Coca-Cola World Ranking granted them direct access to the final mini-league from which the top three nations could progress to Qatar.

Coach Gregg Berhalter's men enjoyed a solid start with draws against El Salvador and Canada, plus victories over Honduras and Jamaica. Defeat in Panama was followed by important wins over Costa Rica and Mexico. A 5-1 victory over Panama in the penultimate match effectively assured the USA the third and last certain qualifying spot ahead of Costa Rica. Christian Pulisic, from Chelsea in the English Premier League, scored a hat-trick including two penalties.

Berhalter wasted little time celebrating qualification. Immediately, he switched his focus to progressing beyond the first-round group stage in Qatar. Berhalter, who played in the 2002 finals and was an unused substitute in 2006, said: "The starting point for us will be getting out of the group. Once you do that, it's knockout, single elimination, so anything can happen."

The most successful USA World Cup campaign to date was at the inaugural finals in Uruguay in 1930. They won their group but were then beaten 6-0 by Argentina in the semi-finals. The first round was the end of the road in 1934 and 1950 and the USA then went nine successive World Cups without qualifying for the finals. Finally, a long-awaited revival was sparked by the rise of competing new professional

ABOVE: The USA are back, after missing out in 2018.

✴ ONES TO WATCH

DeANDRE YEDLIN
BORN: 9 JULY 1993
CLUB: INTER MIAMI

DeAndre Yedlin was born and brought up in Seattle. He played youth soccer with Seattle Sounders and the college game with University of Akron in Ohio. The wing-back made his Major League Soccer debut with Seattle in 2013 and transferred a year later to Tottenham Hotspur in the English Premier League. Later, he played for Sunderland, Newcastle and Galatasaray in Turkey before returning home early this year to Inter Miami. He made his senior national team debut in 2014 and played months later at the World Cup finals in Brazil.

CHRISTIAN PULISIC
BORN: 18 SEPTEMBER 1998
CLUB: CHELSEA (ENG)

Christian Pulisic made history as the first American to win the UEFA Champions League with Chelsea in 2021. The free-scoring winger had joined the London club from Borussia Dortmund with whom he had won the German cup in 2017. Pulisic, born in Hershey, Pennsylvania, played and scored at every US youth level and made his senior national-team debut in March 2016. He helped lead them to the final of the 2019 Concacaf Gold Cup and to win the inaugural 2019-2020 Concacaf Nations League. Three times he has been voted U.S. Soccer Male Athlete of the Year.

RECORD AT PREVIOUS TOURNAMENTS

◆ ◆ ◆ ◆ ◆ ◆ ◆

1930	SEMI-FINALS
1934	FIRST ROUND
1938	DID NOT ENTER
1950	FIRST ROUND
1954	DID NOT QUALIFY
1958	DID NOT QUALIFY
1962	DID NOT QUALIFY
1966	DID NOT QUALIFY
1970	DID NOT QUALIFY
1974	DID NOT QUALIFY
1978	DID NOT QUALIFY
1982	DID NOT QUALIFY
1986	DID NOT QUALIFY
1990	FIRST ROUND
1994	ROUND OF 16
1998	FIRST ROUND
2002	QUARTER-FINALS
2006	FIRST ROUND
2010	ROUND OF 16
2014	ROUND OF 16
2018	DID NOT QUALIFY

leagues in the 1960s and 1970s, the success of the women's national team in attracting an enthusiastic new domestic audience and the outstanding hosting of the men's 1994 FIFA World Cup™ finals.

That tournament remains the record-holder in attendance terms. No World Cup before or since can match the aggregate total of 3.5m for an event that featured 24 teams, compared with the 32 that have appeared since 1998.

The U.S. Soccer Federation hired World Cup veteran Bora Milutinović as their coach. He led them, in 1991, to a first major international honour in the Concacaf Championship. Milutinović benefited from the unique creation of "Team America" on to which he grafted a number of players with experience of club football in Europe. They defeated a talented Colombia in the group stage of the 1994 World Cup and lost only 1-0 to Brazil in the second round. Team USA were eliminated in the first-round group stage in 1990 and 1998, but reached the round of 16 as hosts in 1994.

Eight years later, in 2002, top domestic club coach Bruce Arena guided the US to the quarter-finals of the World Cup, their best placing since 1930. Along the way, they defeated regional arch-rivals Mexico 2-0 before falling 1-0 to eventual runners-up Germany. The adventure ended in the round of 16 in 2010 and 2014.

The USA failed to qualify for the finals in Russia in 2018, but that did not deter US fans from being among the most eager purchasers of tickets for the next tournament in Qatar – the US football family was among the top three foreign applicants when the opening ticket sales window closed in January.

FIFA WORLD CUP
Qatar2022

WALES

Wales have appeared only once at the finals, progressing to the quarter-finals in Sweden in 1958 before losing to eventual champions Brazil. They are now trying to repeat history, under the inspiration of stars such as Gareth Bale and Aaron Ramsey.

COACH
ROBERT PAGE

ONES TO WATCH

GARETH BALE
BORN: 16 JULY 1989
CLUB: REAL MADRID (SPA)

AARON RAMSEY
BORN: 26 DECEMBER 1990
CLUB: RANGERS (SCO)

The *Red Dragons* had been drawn in a challenging qualifying group, which included Belgium and the Czech Republic. The winners would go directly to Qatar with the runners-up entering the play-offs.

Wales opened their campaign with a 3-1 defeat in Belgium, but recovered with a 1-0 home win over the Czech Republic with a late goal from Daniel James. The Leeds man was on target again in an equally important 2-2 draw against the Czech Republic in Prague. Thus, when the last matchday kicked off, Wales needed one point at home to Belgium to clinch runners-up spot even if the Czechs defeated Estonia.

Kevin De Bruyne put Belgium ahead, but Kieffer Moore equalised later in the first half, and the 1-1 draw secured the crucial home advantage in the play-off semi-finals against Austria. Ramsey was Wales' three-goal leading marksman in the group.

A tense play-off semi-final against Austria ended in a 2-1 win for Wales, courtesy of two superb goals from Bale at the Cardiff City Stadium. Their fans had to endure a nervy finale. Wales conceded a late goal to Marcel Sabitzer and needed resolute defending and the reflexes of goalkeeper Wayne Hennessey to claim the victory, which sent them into the play-off final against Scotland or Ukraine.

The Football Association of Wales is one of the oldest in the world, founded in 1876. They have competed consistently in the qualifying stages of both the FIFA World Cup and UEFA European Championship. Bale's brilliance led them to the semi-finals of the EURO 2016 in France and the round of 16 in last year's rescheduled 2020 finals.

ABOVE: Wales last reached the finals in 1958.

UKRAINE

Ukraine's quarter-finals appearance in 2006, led by the great Andriy Shevchenko, is their best performance to date.

COACH
OLEKSANDR PETRAKOV

ONES TO WATCH

ANDRIY YARMOLENKO
BORN: 23 OCTOBER 1989
CLUB: WEST HAM UNITED (ENG)

OLEKSANDR ZINCHENKO
BORN: 15 DECEMBER 1996
CLUB: MANCHESTER CITY (ENG)

They have also appeared in the last three finals tournaments of the UEFA European Championship. At last year's rescheduled UEFA EURO 2020, Ukraine defeated Sweden 2-1 after extra time in a dramatic tie in the round of 16 before losing to England in the quarter-finals.

In the World Cup qualifying competition to reach Qatar, the Ukrainians were drawn in European Group D along with reigning world champions France. They drew both matches against the French 1-1, away in Saint-Denis and home in Kyiv to complete their eight-game programme unbeaten. However, they secured the all-important runners-up place only by winning their last game away to Bosnia and Herzegovina. Second-half goals from Oleksandr Zinchenko and Artem Dovbyk lifted Ukraine above Finland and into the play-off semi-finals.

Ukraine's leading group scorers were Roman Yaremchuk, with three goals and Andriy Yarmolenko, with two goals.

ABOVE: Ukraine hope to repeat 2006.

SCOTLAND

Scotland made history by contesting the first formal international match in 1872, but have yet to progress beyond the first round at the finals.

COACH
STEVE CLARKE

ONES TO WATCH

CRAIG GORDON
BORN: 31 DECEMBER 1982
CLUB: HEARTS (SCO)

ANDREW ROBERTSON
BORN: 11 MARCH 1994
CLUB: LIVERPOOL (ENG)

The Tartan Army of supporters have seen the Scots reach the finals of the FIFA World Cup on eight occasions. Their first appearance was in 1954 and their last in 1998 in France, when Scotland fell short of progress after losing narrowly to Brazil in the opening match. A proud memory was a 3-2 win over the Netherlands in the 1978 finals when Archie Gemmill scored one of the finest goals seen in the finals.

Scotland reached the semi-finals of the qualifying play-offs for the right to play in Qatar by finishing runners-up in European Group F. They placed four points behind Denmark, but safely clear of Israel with a game to spare. A 2-0 win over the Danes in their last match was too late to affect the standings. Lyndon Dykes and John McGinn were Scotland's top scorers with four goals each.

ABOVE: Scotland played eight times at the finals.

FIFA WORLD CUP
Qatar2022™

ARGENTINA

Argentina's record of producing a never-ending stream of outstanding footballers has been rewarded with two victories in the FIFA World Cup in 1978 and 1986. Lionel Messi, now in his mid-30s, is still one of the world's greatest players.

COACH
LIONEL SCALONI

Lionel Scaloni was born on 16 May 1978 and was thus five weeks old when Argentina won the World Cup for the first time. He later tasted World Cup drama as a player himself in 2006. At club level, after stints with Newell's Old Boys and Estudiantes in his homeland, Scaloni played in midfield or at full-back for Deportivo La Coruña, Racing Santander and Mallorca in Spain, as well as Lazio and Atalanta in Italy – plus, briefly, West Ham United in the English Premier League. Scaloni turned to coaching as assistant to Jorge Sampaoli with Sevilla and then with the national team. He was handed the top job in 2018 and led Argentina to third place at the CONMEBOL *Copa América* in 2019 and to victory in 2021.

Messi, as captain and attacking inspiration, led Argentina to qualification for the FIFA World Cup 2022 in Qatar, which was achieved with six matches remaining, courtesy of a 0-0 draw against Brazil. His goal haul included the only strike of the game in the *Albiceleste*'s opener against Ecuador, a hat-trick against Bolivia and the opening goal against Uruguay.

Reaching the World Cup for the 13th time in a row built on the success that Messi and his team-mates had achieved four months earlier in winning the CONMEBOL *Copa América*. That was the country's first major title at senior level since the FIFA Confederations Cup in 1992. Coach Lionel Scaloni said: "This has been a magnificent year. To win the *Copa América* and then qualify for the World Cup unbeaten was a dream come true."

Argentina's football history is not only a proud one but a long one. The British brought football to the country in the 1860s and, picking up where a short-lived predecessor had left off, the Argentinian Football Association was founded in 1893 by an English schoolteacher, Alexander Hutton. It set up a league the same year and in 1902, the national side met Uruguay in the first official international match to be staged outside Great Britain.

Professionalism was adopted in the early 1930s, when the Buenos Aires giants River Plate and Boca Juniors emerged as dominant forces of the domestic club game.

Argentina were runners-up to Uruguay at the 1928 Olympic Games and then lost 4-2 to their neighbours in the 1930 World Cup final. They were knocked out at the first time of asking in 1934 and were absent from

ABOVE: Argentina have won the World Cup twice, in 1978 and 1986.

⬟ ONES TO WATCH

ÁNGEL DI MARÍA
BORN: 14 FEBRUARY 1988
CLUB: PARIS SAINT-GERMAIN (FRA)

Di María was a key member of the Argentina team who finished runners-up to Germany in Brazil in 2014. A versatile winger, he also scored Argentina's Olympic gold medal-winning goal against Nigeria in 2008. Di María's club career began with hometown Rosario Central before moving to Benfica, Real Madrid, Manchester United and Paris Saint-Germain. He featured at the 2010, 2014 and 2018 editions of the World Cup. During the 2019 CONMEBOL *Copa América*, he became only the sixth Argentinian to reach 100 caps.

LAUTARO MARTÍNEZ
BORN: 22 AUGUST 1997
CLUB: INTER MILAN (ITA)

Lautaro Martínez scored important goals in the qualifying wins over Bolivia and Peru (home and away), as well as Colombia, Venezuela and Uruguay. Those strikes enhanced the reputation he was acquiring in Italy's *Serie A* for Inter, with whom he won the league title in 2021. Martínez had joined Inter from Racing Club in 2018. He played for Argentina at the FIFA U-20 World Cup in 2017 and made his senior international debut a year later. He helped the *Albiceleste* finish third at the CONMEBOL *Copa América* in 2019 and win the tournament in 2021.

RECORD AT PREVIOUS TOURNAMENTS

1930	RUNNERS-UP
1934	FIRST ROUND
1938	WITHDREW
1950	WITHDREW
1954	DID NOT ENTER
1958	FIRST ROUND
1962	FIRST ROUND
1966	QUARTER-FINALS
1970	DID NOT QUALIFY
1974	SECOND ROUND
1978	CHAMPIONS
1982	SECOND ROUND
1986	CHAMPIONS
1990	RUNNERS-UP
1994	SECOND ROUND
1998	QUARTER-FINALS
2002	FIRST ROUND
2006	QUARTER-FINALS
2010	QUARTER-FINALS
2014	RUNNERS-UP
2018	SECOND ROUND

the next three tournaments while continuing to produce great players, including Alfredo Di Stéfano and Omar Sívori. Many members of these later generations maintained the reputation of Argentinian football with their achievements on behalf of clubs in Spain and Italy.

The *Albiceleste* returned to the World Cup in 1958. Both then and in 1962, they failed to progress, while their run in 1966 was ended with a quarter-final defeat by hosts England.

World Cup success was finally achieved in 1978, when Argentina hosted the competition. In the final, a team coached by César Luis Menotti defeated the Netherlands 3-1 after extra time. Striker Mario Kempes was the tournament's top scorer with six goals, including two in the final. Argentina celebrated World Cup glory again eight years later when captain Diego Maradona inspired them to a 3-2 victory over West Germany at the Estadio Azteca in Mexico City.

Argentina were runners-up in 1990 and then again in Brazil eight years ago, when Messi's consolation was to win the adidas Golden Ball as the player of the tournament. In Russia, four years later, their World Cup campaign ended with a 4-3 loss to eventual champions France in the round of 16.

Argentina were cheered on from the stands by Maradona, whose death in 2020, at the age of 60, was mourned throughout the football world. The *Albiceleste*, at the time, were already four matches into their qualifying campaign for Qatar. Successors ambitious to follow in Maradona's glorious World Cup footsteps included not only veterans Messi, Ángel Di María and defender Nicolás Otamendi but newcomers such as Lautaro Martínez, too.

SAUDI ARABIA

FIFA WORLD CUP
Qatar2022

Saudi Arabia's status as a force in Asian football has been underlined by their appearance at the FIFA World Cup finals for the second time in succession, and sixth time in all. The *Green Falcons* have been Asian champions on three occasions too.

COACH
HERVÉ RENARD

Herve Renard, born on 30 September, 1968, is a French coach who has made his name with African national teams. As a youngster he had played for AS Cannes, alongside Zinedine Zidane. He worked briefly in management in China, England (with Cambridge United), Vietnam and France before becoming coach of Zambia in 2008. Later he guided Zambia to victory in the African Cup of Nations in 2012. Renard became the first coach to win the African crown with different nations with Côte d'Ivoire in 2015. He guided Morocco to the FIFA World Cup finals in 2018 and was appointed by Saudi Arabia the following year.

Four years ago, the Saudis failed to progress beyond the group stage, and the national team must look back to their finals debut in 1994 for their best performance.

In the USA, they reached the round of 16 before losing narrowly to Sweden. They defeated Belgium and Morocco in the group stage and Saeed Al-Owairan scored, against the Belgians, what remains one of the most outstanding individual goals in the finals' modern history. The attacking midfielder pierced the heart of the Belgian midfield by accelerating from inside his own half before firing home.

The Saudi Arabian Football Federation was founded in 1956 and celebrated initial honours by winning the 1984 and 1988 Asian titles. They maintained the good work by investing heavily in foreign coaching expertise and building the King Fahd Stadium in Riyadh, which hosted the FIFA Confederations Cup in 1993.

That commitment to the game paid off in another Asian title in 1996 amid a hat-trick of successive appearances at the World Cup finals in 1994, 1998 and 2002. In the latter tournament in Japan and Korea Republic, the Saudi Arabians were unable to record either a point or a goal. The association promised a major overhaul of the domestic game, which has been rewarded with an increasingly influential role in the Asian game both on and off the pitch.

Saudi history includes some of the most iconic players in the Asian game in Mohamed Al-Deayea and Majed Abdullah. Al-Deayea kept goal in four FIFA World Cups and, between 1993 and 2006, made 178 appearances, a world record for a goalkeeper.

At the other end of the pitch, Saudi Arabia were inspired by Abdullah, the so-called "Pelé of the Desert."

ABOVE: Saudi Arabia qualified with one game still to play.

⬖ ONES TO WATCH

SALEM AL-DAWSARI
BORN: 19 AUGUST 1991
CLUB: AL-HILAL

Salem Al-Dawsari is a winger who scores important goals. He celebrated his first international appearance in Saudi Arabia's ultimately unsuccessful qualifying competition for the 2014 FIFA World Cup™. Four years later he played in the finals in Russia and scored a late winning goal in a 2-1 group victory over Egypt. Al-Dawsari had a brief loan spell with Villarreal before returning to Al-Hilal. He scored an important goal in their 2019 AFC Champions League Final victory over Urawa Red Diamonds. Al-Hilal went on to reach the semi-finals of the FIFA Club World Cup 2019™.

YASSER AL-SHAHRANI
BORN: 25 MAY 1992
CLUB: AL-HILAL

Yasser Al-Shahrani's international competitive experience stretches back to goalscoring appearances in the FIFA U-20 World Cup 2011. Seven years later, he had graduated to playing left-back for Saudi Arabia in the opening match against hosts Russia in Moscow. Now he totals more than 60 matches for his country. Al-Shahrani, at club level, made his name with Al-Qadsiah before joining Al-Hilal in 2012. He has won four league titles with Al-Hilal, has had seven successes in various domestic cup competitions and two triumphs in the AFC Asian Champions League.

RECORD AT PREVIOUS TOURNAMENTS

1930	DID NOT EXIST
1934	NOT IN MEMBERSHIP
1938	NOT IN MEMBERSHIP
1950	NOT IN MEMBERSHIP
1954	NOT IN MEMBERSHIP
1958	NOT IN MEMBERSHIP
1962	DID NOT ENTER
1966	DID NOT ENTER
1970	DID NOT ENTER
1974	DID NOT ENTER
1978	DID NOT QUALIFY
1982	DID NOT QUALIFY
1986	DID NOT QUALIFY
1990	DID NOT QUALIFY
1994	ROUND OF 16
1998	FIRST ROUND
2002	FIRST ROUND
2006	FIRST ROUND
2010	DID NOT QUALIFY
2014	DID NOT QUALIFY
2018	FIRST ROUND

Abdullah ranks among the greatest marksmen in national-team football history after scoring 115 goals for his country during an era in which he was voted Asian Footballer of the Year on three occasions.

The baton has been passed on to current successors, such as defender Yasser Al-Shahrani, midfielders Salman Al-Faraj, Salem Al-Dawsari and Fahad Al-Muwallad.

Saudi Arabia's progress towards the World Cup finals in neighbouring Qatar began in the second round, which also doubled in the AFC Asian Cup qualifying competition. Rivals in Group D were Uzbekistan, Palestine, Singapore and Yemen, but none of them caused the Saudis any major problems.

The immediate challenge was to progress by topping the group and they achieved this in style by winning six of their eight games and drawing the other two. They completed the schedule undefeated and five points clear of runners-up Uzbekistan. Al-Dawsari was second-leading marksman in the group with five goals, followed by Al-Faraj and Al-Muwallad with four apiece.

The third-round group was a difficult one, including Japan and Australia as well as China PR, Oman and Vietnam. They began positively with wins over Vietnam and Oman. Then, most importantly, the Saudis defeated Japan 1-0 in Jeddah with a 71st-minute goal from Firas Al-Buraikan. Their only defeat was by 2-0 away to Japan before a 0-0 draw against China PR in Sharjah – which officially counted as an away game – that secured their place in the finals with one game still to play.

The 28-year-old forward Saleh Al-Shehri had been their four-goal leading marksman, adding to his three strikes in the second-round group.

MEXICO

Mexico fly to Qatar with coach Gerardo Martino and his players are determined to improve on a proud record that has seen them reach the round of 16 on their last seven successive appearances at the pinnacle of the international game.

COACH
GERARDO MARTINO

Gerardo Martino, born on 20 November 1962, is an Argentinian coach who has been in charge of Mexico since 2019. As a player, he was a league title winner in Argentina with Newell's Old Boys and then, as a coach, won further national titles in Paraguay and Argentina as well as the MLS Cup in the USA, plus both the Spanish cup and supercup with Barcelona. Martino guided Mexico to victory shortly after taking over at the Concacaf Gold Cup in 2019 and to runners-up spot last year. He was voted South American coach of the year in 2007 and then Major League Soccer coach of the year in 2018.

Only four nations – Brazil, Germany, Italy and Argentina – have appeared in the World Cup finals more often than Mexico, whose latest adventure began in the third round mini-league of the Concacaf qualifying system. Their status in the world ranking had earned them inclusion among the five nations that were granted a bye beyond the opening rounds.

The Octagonal, thus labelled for the eight teams competing, was played between September 2021 and March this year.

Mexico were unbeaten in their opening six matches, which included an important victory away to Costa Rica. However, they then suffered a double setback on losing by 2-0 away to the USA in Cincinnati and by 2-1 to Canada in Edmonton. The latter match was remarkable for the conditions in which it was played. The temperature of -9°C made it the coldest match in the history of Mexican national-team football.

Martino's men appeared in danger of a third successive defeat, when they were one goal down to Jamaca in Kingston, with less than ten minutes remaining. Two goals in a minute from Henry Martin and Alexis Vega provided an escape to victory. Mexico thus kicked off their final group match needing a win or draw against El Salvador to ensure their presence in Qatar. An early goal from Uriel Antuna and then a penalty from Raúl Jiménez delivered a 2-0 victory to spark qualification celebrations in the Estadio Azteca.

The cradle of football in Mexico is Pachuca in the state of Hidalgo. The game was introduced by tin miners from the county of Cornwall in the south-west of England. CF Pachuca was founded in 1901 and is now one of the most successful clubs in Latin America. The national association was founded

ABOVE: Mexico are making their 17th appearance at the finals.

GUILLERMO OCHOA
BORN: 13 JULY 1985
CLUB: AMÉRICA

Guillermo Ochoa is the captain of both the Mexican national team and his club, América. He has played more than 120 times for *El Tri* since making his debut in 2005. Ochoa has featured in Mexico's squads at the four successive FIFA World Cups and has been a Concacaf Gold Cup winner on four occasions. He also helped Mexico win the bronze medal at the rescheduled 2020 Olympics last year in Tokyo. Ochoa spent seven years with Club América before moving to Ajaccio in France, Malaga and Granada in Spain, and Standard Liège with whom he won the Belgian cup.

RAÚL JIMÉNEZ
BORN: 5 MAY 1991
CLUB: WOLVERHAMPTON WANDERERS (ENG)

Centre-forward Raúl Jiménez has been a virtual ever-present in Mexico's squads in the last ten years at the FIFA World Cups, Concacaf Gold Cups and Olympic Games. He made his name with Club América before joining Atlético Madrid in 2014. Next came four years and five major trophies with Benfica before a further transfer to Wolverhampton Wanderers in the English Premier League. Jiménez returned to maintain his goalscoring form with club and country after suffering a fractured skull against Arsenal in late 2020.

RECORD AT PREVIOUS TOURNAMENTS

1930	FIRST ROUND
1934	DID NOT QUALIFY
1938	WITHDREW
1950	FIRST ROUND
1954	FIRST ROUND
1958	FIRST ROUND
1962	FIRST ROUND
1966	FIRST ROUND
1970	QUARTER-FINALS
1974	DID NOT QUALIFY
1978	FIRST ROUND
1982	DID NOT QUALIFY
1986	QUARTER-FINALS
1990	SUSPENDED
1994	ROUND OF 16
1998	ROUND OF 16
2002	ROUND OF 16
2006	ROUND OF 16
2010	ROUND OF 16
2014	ROUND OF 16
2018	ROUND OF 16

in 1922 and joined FIFA in 1929, just in time for Mexico to feature among the pioneers who contested the inaugural World Cup in Uruguay in 1930.

That was the first of 16 appearances in the finals. Mexico's proudest performances were in 1970 and 1986 when, as hosts each time, they reached the quarter-finals. Last time out, in Russia in 2018, *El Tri* reached the round of 16 before being eliminated after a 2-0 defeat by Brazil in Samara.

Mexico are one of the most dominant forces of Central and North American football. They will be joint hosts of the FIFA World Cup 2026™, with Canada and the USA, and have won the Concacaf Gold Cup on a record 11 occasions. They also reached the quarter-finals of the centenary edition of the CONMEBOL *Copa América* in 2016 and then the semi-finals of the FIFA Confederations Cup in Russia in 2017.

Mexico's club game has produced outstanding individuals. Goalkeeper Antonio Carbajal played in a then record five World Cups between 1954 and 1966, while centre-forward Hugo Sánchez claimed more than 500 goals in a high-scoring career that included 11 seasons in Spanish football with Atlético and then Real Madrid. Sánchez scored 29 goals in 58 appearances for Mexico, whom he led to the FIFA World Cup 1986™ quarter-finals.

More recent heroes have included penalty-saving goalkeeper Guillermo Ochoa, long-serving captains Claudio Suárez and Rafael Márquez, plus forwards Javier Hernández and Oribe Peralta. Suárez, nicknamed *El Emperador*, is Mexico's record international with 177 caps between 1992 and 2006. Hernández is *El Tri*'s record marksman, while Peralta was the two-goal hero of Mexico's Olympic Games triumph in 2012.

POLAND

The goalscoring genius of FIFA award-winning captain Robert Lewandowski offers Poland confidence of progressing beyond the group stage of the World Cup for the first time since reaching the round of 16 in 1986.

COACH
CZESŁAW MICHNIEWICZ

Czesław Michniewicz, born on 12 February 1970, had a baptism of fire after being appointed national-team coach last January. His immediate task was to guide Poland through the World Cup European play-offs, which he accomplished successfully. Michniewicz had almost two decades' experience behind him. His coaching record included ten clubs as well as three years in charge of the national U-21 team between 2017 and 2020. His club record includes league championship success with Zagłębie Lubin and Legia Warsaw, as well as cup success with Lech Poznań and Legia, plus super cup victories with Lech and Zagłębie.

The qualifying draw had seen Poland placed in a challenging European Group I along with England, Albania, Hungary, Andorra and San Marino. Initial results were mixed. Poland drew 3-3 in Hungary, defeated Andorra 3-0, but then lost 2-1 away to England at Wembley. That left them outside of the crucial top two slots when the campaign had to be interrupted for the rescheduled UEFA EURO 2020 finals.

Again, the Poles' results failed to match their potential. They finished fourth in a first-round table behind Sweden, Spain and Slovakia.

Disappointment rekindled Poland's determination for their World Cup qualifying campaign. Some aggressive attacking football brought 16 goals in their initial three matches. Poland held group leaders England to a 1-1 draw at home in Warsaw and were guaranteed runners-up spot even before losing 2-1 at home to Hungary in their last match.

UEFA's play-off system cast Poland into Path B, but before they could return to action, they had to appoint a new national-team coach. Portuguese Paulo Sousa stepped down after the group stage and was replaced for the play-offs, at short notice, by a former U-21 team manager in Czesław Michniewicz.

Poland had been due to face Russia in the semi-finals, but events in Ukraine saw Russian teams suspended from international competitions by FIFA. Thus, Poland were awarded a bye into the play-off final against the same Swedes who had beaten them 3-2 in the European finals. Now Poland turned the tables with a 2-0 victory in Warsaw. Lewandowski scored the first goal to add to the eight he had registered in the group phase.

ABOVE: Poland beat Sweden in the European play-off finals.

ONES TO WATCH

KAMIL GLIK
BORN: 3 FEBRUARY 1988
CLUB: BENEVENTO (ITA)

Kamil Glik has proved himself as one of the most consistently reliable central defenders in European club football. He was also a pillar of Poland's national team at the UEFA European Championship finals of 2016 and 2020 and at the FIFA World Cup in 2018 in Russia. He was spotted as a teenager in his home town and had two seasons in Spain with Real Madrid C before returning home, and then playing in Italy and France where he was a league champion with Monaco. Glik made his Poland senior debut in January 2010, celebrating the occasion with a goal against Thailand.

WOJCIECH SZCZĘSNY
BORN: 18 APRIL 1990
CLUB: JUVENTUS (ITA)

Wojciech Szczęsny has won a string of club honours in a 13-year goalkeeping career at top level in both England and Italy. He has won the Italian *Serie A* crown three times with Juventus as well as the *Copa Italia* and *Supercoppa* twice each. Previously, he had won the FA Cup twice during eight years in English football with Arsenal. Szczęsny had joined the London club as a teenager from Legia Warsaw, in his home city. He made his senior Poland debut in 2009 and played for his country in the finals of the UEFA EURO in 2012 and 2016, as well as in the FIFA World Cup in 2018.

RECORD AT PREVIOUS TOURNAMENTS

1930	DID NOT ENTER
1934	DID NOT ENTER
1938	FIRST ROUND
1950	DID NOT ENTER
1954	DID NOT ENTER
1958	DID NOT QUALIFY
1962	DID NOT QUALIFY
1966	DID NOT QUALIFY
1970	DID NOT QUALIFY
1974	THIRD PLACE
1978	SECOND ROUND
1982	THIRD PLACE
1986	ROUND OF 16
1990	DID NOT QUALIFY
1994	DID NOT QUALIFY
1998	DID NOT QUALIFY
2002	FIRST ROUND
2006	FIRST ROUND
2010	DID NOT QUALIFY
2014	DID NOT QUALIFY
2018	FIRST ROUND

The Poles thus fly to Qatar celebrating just over a century of national-team football. The state had attained independence in 1918, the football association was founded a year later and the national team played their first international in 1921. Poland joined FIFA in 1923 and made their debut at the World Cup finals in 1938. They were eliminated by Brazil in the first round, but made history in dramatic fashion when Ernest Wilimowski became the first player to score a hat-trick for the losing side.

That proved Poland's last appearance at the pinnacle of the game for more than three decades. A revival was signalled by the progress of Górnik Zabrze to the UEFA European Cup Winners' Cup final in 1969. Three years later, Poland won the football gold medal at the Olympic Games in Munich, with a side starring forward Włodzimierz Lubański, playmaker Kazimierz Deyna and left-winger Robert Gadocha.

This trio were joined at the 1974 FIFA World Cup finals by striker Gregorz Lato and goalkeeper Jan Tomaszewski. Lato was the competition's seven-goal leading scorer as Poland finished third, defeating outgoing champions Brazil 1-0 for the honour. They reached the second round in 1978 and then, in 1982, placed third once more. A team led by a new attacking star in Zbigniew Boniek defeated France 3-2 in the play-off.

Political upheavals in the late 1980s brought change and challenge for the domestic game. These were reflected in the national team failing to progress beyond the group stage at the World Cups of 2002 and 2006 and even at UEFA EURO 2012, despite being co-hosts with Ukraine. Poland were absent from the World Cups of 2010 and 2014, but regained their place in Russia four years ago.

FRANCE

France will become only the third nation to win the FIFA World Cup twice in succession if Qatar sees them repeat their 2018 triumph. This highest standard of excellence had been set by Italy in 1934 and 1938, and was then matched by Brazil in 1958 and 1962.

COACH
DIDIER DESCHAMPS

Didier Deschamps, born on 15 October 1968, ranks among the most successful national-team coaches of all time. He was also one of the international game's most successful players. The former Marseille, Juventus and Chelsea midfielder captained France to World Cup victory in 1998 and then matched that achievement as coach at Russia 2018. Deschamps had captained *Les Bleus* to UEFA EURO success in 2000 before coaching Monaco, Juventus and Marseille en route to taking up the France role in 2012. He also guided his team to the UEFA EURO 2016 final, where they lost to Portugal after extra time.

Les Bleus bring to the World Cup finals not only the all-round talents of a battle-hardened squad of players, but the pride of a nation that boasts a historic connection to football's most prestigious tournament.

Frenchman Jules Rimet was the long-time FIFA President who oversaw the creation of the World Cup and ensured that France were one of the four European nations who contested the first final tournament. Not only that, but Frenchman Lucien Laurent scored the first goal in World Cup history in Uruguay back in 1930.

In 1938, France were only the second European nation to host the tournament and, 20 years later in Sweden, centre-forward Just Fontaine set a record, which still stands, of 13 goals in one tournament. His goals, the majority of which were created by his legendary strike partner Raymond Kopa, led France to third place.

A team led by Michel Platini finished third again in 1986 before their successors, inspired by coach Aimé Jacquet and captain Deschamps, gave France their first World Cup trophy in 1998. The hosts defeated Brazil 3-0 in the final in the Stade de France, with two goals from Zinedine Zidane and one from Emmanuel Petit. Two years later, they added the European crown to their world title.

France reached the World Cup final again in Germany in 2006. They took an early lead through a Zidane penalty, but were pegged back to 1-1 by Italy and lost the penalty shoot-out. Coach Raymond Domenech was succeeded by Laurent Blanc and then Deschamps. The latter guided France to the quarter-finals in Brazil in 2014, to the runners-up spot as the hosts of UEFA EURO 2016, and then to World Cup glory two years later.

Deschamps' reign has been impressively consistent. He has built

ABOVE: France will be defending their FIFA World Cup crown.

✳ ONES TO WATCH

HUGO LLORIS
BORN: 26 DECEMBER 1986
CLUB: TOTTENHAM HOTSPUR (ENG)

Hugo Lloris joined an exclusive club when, as captain of France, he lifted the World Cup four years ago. The only previous winning goalkeeper captains had been Italy's Gianpiero Combi and Dino Zoff, and Spain's Iker Casillas. Lloris's consistency over the past decade has made him one of the finest goalkeepers in the world. He was a European U-19 champion in 2005 and made the first of his 100+ senior national-team appearances three years later. Now a veteran of three World Cups, Lloris joined Tottenham Hotspur from Lyon in 2012.

N'GOLO KANTÉ
BORN: 29 MARCH 1991
CLUB: CHELSEA (ENG)

N'Golo Kanté is the midfield heartbeat of the French national team. He began his career in the French lower divisions with Boulogne and Caen before taking up a starring role in Leicester City's surprise English Premier League success in 2016. A transfer to Chelsea brought further club success at national and international level and his crowning glory was World Cup stardom with France in Russia. Kanté had made his senior debut for *Les Bleus* only two years earlier when he featured in the squad that finished as the UEFA EURO runners-up.

RECORD AT PREVIOUS TOURNAMENTS

1930	FIRST ROUND
1934	FIRST ROUND
1938	QUARTER-FINALS
1950	WITHDREW
1954	FIRST ROUND
1958	THIRD PLACE
1962	DID NOT QUALIFY
1966	FIRST ROUND
1970	DID NOT QUALIFY
1974	DID NOT QUALIFY
1978	FIRST ROUND
1982	FOURTH PLACE
1986	THIRD PLACE
1990	DID NOT QUALIFY
1994	DID NOT QUALIFY
1998	CHAMPIONS
2002	FIRST ROUND
2006	RUNNERS-UP
2010	FIRST ROUND
2014	QUARTER-FINALS
2018	CHAMPIONS

and rebuilt successful teams in the post-Zidane era that have always played entertaining and positive football, and qualified for the finals of every major tournament. The nucleus of the team that triumphed in Moscow four years ago provided the foundations for the latest qualifying campaign.

Les Bleus disappointed home fans in the Stade de France with a 1-1 draw against Ukraine in their opening match in European Group D, before gathering pace with away victories by 2-0 in Kazakhstan, and 1-0 against Bosnia and Herzegovina. Attention then switched to the postponed UEFA

EURO finals, where France topped a group including Germany and Portugal, before losing on penalties to Switzerland after an exciting 3-3 draw in the round of 16.

A hangover from that outcome, combined with a number of injuries, appeared to affect the resumption of the World Cup effort. France drew 1-1 with Bosnia and Herzegovina, and then Ukraine again before securing a place in Qatar with an 8-0 home win over Kazakhstan. Kylian Mbappé scored his first international hat-trick inside 32 minutes, and added a fourth towards the end of the match.

Karim Benzema also contributed two goals in the second half and there were also strikes from Adrien Rabiot and Antoine Griezmann. Mbappé said: "We wanted to give ourselves a chance to defend our title. Even for those who have played in it and won it, it's an ultimate dream to play in a World Cup. The fans enjoyed it, so did we."

France finished six points ahead of Ukraine. Griezmann and Finland's Teemu Pukki were the group's leading scorers with six goals apiece. Mbappé ended the qualifying campaign with five goals, including France's second goal in their concluding 2-0 win in Finland.

PERU

Peru are play-off specialists. Their route to the FIFA World Cup finals in Russia four years ago demanded a play-off victory over New Zealand to end a 36-year absence. This time around coach Ricardo Gareca and his players again finished fifth in the South American qualifying mini-league.

COACH
RICARDO GARECA

ONES TO WATCH

YOSHIMAR YOTÚN
BORN: 7 APRIL 1990
CLUB: SPORTING CRISTAL

LUIS ADVÍNCULA
BORN: 2 MARCH 1990
CLUB: BOCA JUNIORS (ARG)

Lima and its clubs have dominated football in Peru ever since the football association was founded there in 1922. The national team made their debut five years later in the CONMEBOL *Copa América* and they won the event on home turf in 1939. Peru have won the CONMEBOL tournament on only one other occasion, in 1975, during the national team's so-called "golden era", when they also qualified three times for the World Cup finals.

Peru appeared at the inaugural tournament in Uruguay in 1930 and so helped create history. But they failed to progress beyond the opening round and did not appear on the grand stage for another 40 years. In Mexico in 1970, a fine side starring all time Peruvian "greats" such as Teófilo Cubillas, Hugo Sotil and Héctor Chumpitaz achieved their finest finish by reaching the quarter-finals.

Chumpitaz, Sotil and Cubillas were still on hand when Peru reached the second round mini-league in 1978 in Argentina. Only Cubillas remained in Spain in 1982.

A new generation made their presence felt at the CONMEBOL *Copa América* in 2015, when they reached the quarter-finals before maintaining momentum by reaching the 2018 World Cup finals. Veterans include defenders Christian Ramos and Luis Advíncula, plus midfielders Yoshimar Yotún and Christian Cueva.

Peru were not certain of the play-off place until the last matchday. They kicked off at home to Paraguay leading Colombia by one point and needing victory. Gianluca Lapadula set Peru on their way after only five minutes and Yotún struck again just before the interval for the essential 2-0 victory.

ABOVE: Peru finished fifth in the South American qualifying group.

UNITED ARAB EMIRATES

The United Arab Emirates have been chasing the dream of a role once more at the FIFA World Cup finals ever since their debut in 1990.

COACH
RODOLFO ARRUABARRENA

ONES TO WATCH

WALID ABBAS
BORN: 11 JUNE 1985
CLUB: SHABAB AL-AHLI

ALI MABKHOUT
BORN: 5 OCTOBER 1990
CLUB: AL JAZIRA

Their only appearance so far ended in the first-round group stage in Italy, but this encouraged steady progress in the domestic game and in Asian competitions. The UAE took third place at the AFC Asian Cup finals in 2015 and were semi-finalists again in 2019.

Argentinian coach Rodolfo Arruabarrena was hired early this year. The UAE had edged out Vietnam by one point to win their second round Group G. Ali Mabkhout was the group's top scorer with 11 goals. The third round ended up with the UAE placed a distant third behind IR Iran and Korea Republic, but three points clear of Iraq to earn the play-off opportunity.

Their most experienced players are defender Walid Abbas and forward Ali Mabkhout. Both have played more than 100 times for the UAE. Abbas made his debut in 2008 and Mabkhout a year later. He is all-time top scorer with more than 70 goals.

ABOVE: UAE have been finalists once.

AUSTRALIA

Australia are the only team that have been champions of two confederations. They won the OFC Nations Cup four times and the AFC Asian Cup in 2015.

COACH
GRAHAM ARNOLD

ONES TO WATCH

TOM ROGIC
BORN: 16 DECEMBER 1992
CLUB: CELTIC (SCO)

TRENT SAINSBURY
BORN: 5 JANUARY 1992
CLUB: KORTRIJK (BEL)

The *Socceroos* have appeared at the FIFA World Cup finals on five occasions, and were ever-present from 2006 to 2018. Their most successful campaign was in 2006 in Germany, when they progressed to the round of 16 before losing to eventual champions Italy.

Australia's journey towards Qatar began with the Asian qualifying second round in which they finished a decisive ten points clear of Kuwait in Group B. Coach Graham Arnold's team won all their eight games with a massive 28-2 aggregate. The third round proved to be a different story.

Saudi Araba and Japan took the top two places in Group B and Australia secured third place and entry to the play-offs by only one point ahead of Oman. A 2-2 draw away to Oman in Muscat proved crucial.

ABOVE: Australia are five-time finalists.

DENMARK

Although Denmark have never reached the last four of the FIFA World Cup, they have contributed massively to the popularity of national-team football. The personality that defines the "Danish Dynamite" spirit has captivated fans everywhere.

COACH
KASPER HJULMAND

Hjulmand, born on 9 April 1972, was denied a long playing career by a serious knee injury when he was only 26. He turned to coaching with Lyngby and then Nordsjælland, whom he led to the *Superliga* title in 2012. This win led him to succeed Thomas Tuchel at Mainz in Germany in 2014. He later returned to Nordsjælland and then succeeded Åge Hareide in 2020 to take charge of a national team that had already qualified for the UEFA EURO finals. Hjulmand's first major international tournament saw him lead Denmark all the way to the semi-finals before losing to England after extra time at Wembley.

The Danes were among the first in continental Europe to take up football and they boast some of the oldest clubs in the world. They enjoyed early success at the Olympic Games in the pre-World Cup era. Winners in 1906 and runners-up in 1908 and 1912, their outstanding players included Nils Middelboe, who later played in England for Chelsea.

A subsequent period in the international shadows ended in the 1970s. A flood of outstanding players – led by 1977 European Footballer of The Year Allan Simonsen – left Denmark to play abroad. In 1976, this led to the end of a ban on "exiles" playing for the national team. Stars such as Simonsen, Michael Laudrup, Preben Elkjær, Jesper Olsen, Morten Olsen and Søren Lerby brought home their top-level experience and the results were dramatic. Suddenly, Denmark were

again a force to be reckoned with on the global stage.

These players and other new stars formed the nucleus of the side that reached the semi-finals of the UEFA EURO in France in 1984, and the round of 16 at the World Cup in Mexico two years later.

A new generation of players – including Michael Laudrup's brother, Brian – then emerged to propel Denmark to the dizzying heights of European champions in 1992. Goals from John Jensen and Kim Vilfort brought a 2-0 victory over Germany in Gothenburg, Sweden, which completed an unexpected success. Their victory was all the more remarkable because Denmark had only been invited to play in the tournament at the last minute, following the removal of Yugoslavia from the finals due to security concerns.

ABOVE: Denmark were four points clear in their qualifying group.

⬣ ONES TO WATCH

KASPER SCHMEICHEL
BORN: 5 NOVEMBER 1986
CLUB: LEICESTER CITY
(ENG)

Schmeichel has followed in the footsteps of his father, Peter, in establishing himself as a key member of Denmark's squad. He played regularly for the U-21s and has won more than 70 senior caps since his debut in 2013. Schmeichel has never played professional club football in Denmark. He began his career with Manchester City and had various spells out on loan in the English lower divisions before joining Leicester City in 2011. His talent and experience were then major contributors to the club's surprise title triumph in the Premier League in 2016.

SIMON KJÆR
BORN: 26 MARCH 1989
CLUB: AC MILAN (ITA)

Kjær is not only a rock in central defence for Denmark, but also an inspiring captain. He began his career with Midtjylland, but a burgeoning reputation quickly prompted widespread interest among other European clubs. Kjær starred in Italy (Palermo, Roma and Atalanta), in Germany (Wolfsburg), in France (Lille), in Turkey (Fenerbahçe) and in Spain (Sevilla) before returning to *Serie A* with Milan in 2020. Kjær was the first to run to the aid of Eriksen in Copenhagen at UEFA EURO 2020 and then boosted team morale in their progress to the semi-finals.

RECORD AT PREVIOUS TOURNAMENTS

1930	DID NOT ENTER
1934	DID NOT ENTER
1938	DID NOT ENTER
1950	DID NOT ENTER
1954	DID NOT ENTER
1958	DID NOT QUALIFY
1962	DID NOT ENTER
1966	DID NOT QUALIFY
1970	DID NOT QUALIFY
1974	DID NOT QUALIFY
1978	DID NOT QUALIFY
1982	DID NOT QUALIFY
1986	ROUND OF 16
1990	DID NOT QUALIFY
1994	DID NOT QUALIFY
1998	QUARTER-FINALS
2002	ROUND OF 16
2006	DID NOT QUALIFY
2010	FIRST ROUND
2014	DID NOT QUALIFY
2018	ROUND OF 16

Denmark subsequently qualified for the World Cup on four occasions and the UEFA EURO five times. The most successful of these campaigns was in 2021, when Denmark reached the semi-finals of the delayed UEFA EURO finals. Their achievement of progressing to the last four was all the more special since they had withstood the shock caused by the cardiac arrest of playmaker Christian Eriksen in their opening game. Captain Simon Kjær and the medical team received awards from UEFA for their swift reaction to the player's collapse shortly before half-time in a game against Finland.

Eriksen had played in all three of Denmark's initial World Cup qualifying ties in March 2021. These brought victories – 2-0 in Israel, 8-0 at home to Moldova then 4-0 in Austria. The UEFA EURO campaign then took priority before Denmark, now without the convalescing Eriksen, resumed World Cup action in September last year.

More victories followed over Scotland, the Faroe Islands (twice), as well as Israel, Moldova and Austria all for a second time. A place at the finals in Qatar was secured with two games to spare after a 1-0 win over Austria in Copenhagen. Joakim Mæhle scored the all-important second-half goal. Captain Kjær said, "We have come a long way already but we have only become hungrier. We built up a crew and a mentality that is incredibly healthy and we have been eager to improve all the time. We share the best with each other and adding that to the quality we have, we can go a long way."

Denmark later lost their final group game 2-0 in Scotland, but still finished four points clear of the Scots, and 11 points ahead of Israel and Austria. Mæhle and Andreas Skov Olsen were Denmark's leading scorers with five goals each.

TUNISIA

Tunisia are appearing in the finals for the sixth time with the ambition of finally progressing beyond the first round. This has been their sticking point on every one of their appearances in the finals since their debut in 1978 and including their campaign four years ago in Russia.

COACH
JALEL KADRI

Jalel Kadri, who was born on 14 December 1971, crowned his 20-year coaching career by leading Tunisia to the quarter-finals of the Africa Cup of Nations and then the FIFA World Cup finals. Kadri had been promoted from assistant during the Africa Cup in January after Mondher Kebaier was taken ill. Kadri was then named formally as the national team manager for the ultimately successful World Cup qualifying showdown against Mali. His previous appointments had included a spell in charge of the U-20s in 2007-2008 and national-team assistant first time around in 2013.

The *Eagles of Carthage* had made history at the 1978 tournament on becoming the first African nation to win at the finals when they defeated Mexico 3-1. That breakthrough helped persuade the world game to increase Africa's presence at the finals from one team to two in Spain in 1982.

Subsequent appearances saw Tunisia fall short in attack, managing only five goals in total on three successive efforts at the finals in 1998, 2002 and 2006. In between they earned rich consolation by recording their only triumph so far in the Africa Cup of Nations. As hosts in 2004, they defeated Morocco 2-1 in the final.

The French had brought football to Tunis and a league was launched in 1921. Simultaneously, Tunisian clubs began competing in an annual North African championship with sides from Algeria and Morocco. Racing Club de Tunis won the inaugural event in 1919.

Racing were also the first domestic league champions. Espérance Sportive of Tunis, destined to become one of the leading clubs in not only Tunisia but African football, won their first league title in 1938.

An unofficial national team competed against neighbours from Algeria, Oran, Constantine and Morocco in the 1930s and 1940s. National selections also played games against France B teams between 1928 and 1956, when Tunisia gained independence. The newly launched football federation joined both FIFA and the African confederation in 1960.

Tunisia subsequently became the first African nation after Egypt to appear at the Olympic Games football tournament. In 1962 they were the first French-speaking North African country to enter the Africa Cup of Nations, finishing third. Three years

ABOVE: Tunisia are appearing for the fifth time in seven World Cups.

WAHBI KHAZRI
BORN: 8 FEBRUARY, 1991
CLUB: SAINT-ÉTIENNE (FRA)

Wahbi Khazri, an attacking midfielder from Corsica, launched his professional career with Bastia. He helped bring them from the third tier to *Ligue 1* then transferred to Bordeaux, England's Sunderland and Rennes before joining Saint-Étienne in 2018. Khazri played once for France at U-21 level, then made his senior competitive debut for Tunisia in 2017. He has scored more than 20 goals in 60-plus appearances. These included outings at the 2018 World Cup and in five Africa Cup of Nations campaigns. He is Tunisia's captain and second top all-time leading marksman.

ALI MAÂLOUL
BORN: 1 JANUARY, 1990
CLUB: AL AHLY (EGY)

Ali Maâloul is one of the most successful Tunisian players of the modern era. The left-back made his national-team debut in 2013 and has made around 80 appearances including both at the FIFA World Cup and Africa Cup of Nations. He made his name with Sfaxien, where he became captain. In 2016, he transferred to leading Egyptian club Al Ahly with whom he has won the CAF Champions League and Super Cup and finished third at the FIFA Club World Cup in 2020 and 2021. Previously, with Sfaxien, he won the CAF Confederation Cup and North African Cup Winners Cup.

RECORD AT PREVIOUS TOURNAMENTS

1930	DID NOT EXIST
1934	DID NOT EXIST
1938	DID NOT EXIST
1950	DID NOT EXIST
1954	DID NOT EXIST
1958	DID NOT ENTER
1962	DID NOT QUALIFY
1966	WITHDREW
1970	DID NOT QUALIFY
1974	DID NOT QUALIFY
1978	FIRST ROUND
1982	DID NOT QUALIFY
1986	DID NOT QUALIFY
1990	DID NOT QUALIFY
1994	DID NOT QUALIFY
1998	FIRST ROUND
2002	FIRST ROUND
2006	FIRST ROUND
2010	DID NOT QUALIFY
2014	DID NOT QUALIFY
2018	FIRST ROUND

later, as hosts, they finished runners-up to Ghana.

Star player was captain and playmaker Majid Chetali, who was coach of the team that made their World Cup finals debut in 1978. The next major era was in the mid-1990s, when Tunisia were the Africa Nations runners-up and reached the finals of the 1998 World Cup under Polish coach Henryk Kasperczak, the first of their three successive appearances. Kasperczak returned in 2015 to build the foundation of a new team who finished third behind eventual semi-finalists Belgium and

England in their group at the 2018 World Cup.

Tunisia launched their qualifying effort for the 2022 finals in September last year with a 3-1 defeat of Equatorial Guinea. This victory proved crucial because, at the end of the group stage, Tunisia finished two points ahead of the *National Thunder*. They clinched progress with a 2-0 victory over Zambia in their final game on goals from Aïssa Laïdouni, Mohamed Dräger and Ali Maâloul.

Before the final round, Tunisia reached the quarter-finals in a remarkable 15th consecutive

appearance at the finals of the Africa Cup of Nations. Then it was into World Cup action against Mali. Tunisia won the first leg by 1-0 in Bamako.

Coach Jalel Kadri, who had been appointed only in January, warned his team before the return about the danger of complacency and they had to work hard to hold on for a goalless draw in front of a 35,000 crowd in Tunis. Tunisia thus celebrated reaching the World Cup finals once again. A relieved Kadri reacted by promising: "We will play with the objective of reaching the second round for the first time in our history."

SPAIN

Spain made history with a historic hat-trick of major trophies when they won the 2010 FIFA World Cup in between European titles in 2008 and 2012. This followed many years in which Spanish football had stood out largely due to the success of its clubs.

COACH
LUIS ENRIQUE

Luis Enrique, born on 8 May 1970, is another in a long line of Spanish national-team coaches who have also been international players. Born in Gijón in north-west Spain, he played for his local club, then Real Madrid and Barcelona as both an inside-forward and full-back. His host of playing honours include a gold medal at the 1992 Olympic Games. Luis Enrique's coaching career took him to Italy's Roma, after which he returned home to Celta and then Barcelona, a team he led to UEFA Champions League success in 2015. He was appointed Spain coach in 2018 and was then reappointed in November 2020 after a six-month break for family reasons.

That said, history and tradition, however magnificent, are worth nothing out on the pitch. Spain were reminded of that eternal football truth in the opening rounds of the FIFA World Cup qualifying competition in March 2021. European Group B saw them held 1-1 at home by Greece before beating Georgia and Kosovo. That left them only one point ahead of Sweden as the competition was interrupted by the pandemic-delayed UEFA EURO finals.

Fate had brought Spain and Sweden together again at the EURO. A goalless draw gave Spain the platform to finish as group runners-up and to progress into the dramatic knockout stages. Victories after extra time against Croatia, and on penalties over Switzerland, fired them to the semi-finals, where they lost a shoot-out to old rivals Italy.

Resumption of the World Cup qualifiers brought renewed pressure, with a 2-1 defeat to Sweden in Stockholm. This was Spain's first World Cup qualifying loss since 1993 and left them trailing the Swedes, who also had a game in hand. However, Sweden lost away to both Greece and Georgia, and Spain capitalised to set up a last-match showdown in Seville.

Spain needed only a draw, while Sweden had to win. Four minutes from the end, Swedish goalkeeper Robin Olsen tipped a Dani Olmo shot onto the bar and Álvaro Morata tapped home the rebound from close range to send Spain into their 12th consecutive World Cup finals.

It is fitting that Spain will be there since they were one of the founding members of FIFA in 1904. The game had gained a foothold in the Basque country in the 1890s through migrant

ABOVE: Spain were world champions in 2010 in South Africa.

✳ ONES TO WATCH

PEDRI
BORN: 25 NOVEMBER 2002
CLUB: BARCELONA

Pedri (Pedro González López) made his presence felt in a remarkable 2021. He had joined Barcelona only the previous year from Las Palmas before helping his club to win the *Copa del Rey* and was named Young Player of the Tournament at UEFA EURO 2020, when he helped Spain to reach the semi-finals. Pedri was also the only Spanish player to be named in the Team of the Tournament. One month later, he went to the Olympic Games in Tokyo, winning a silver medal. Another month later, he was back in European action in the UEFA Champions League.

ÁLVARO MORATA
BORN: 23 OCTOBER 1992
CLUB: ATLÉTICO MADRID

Álvaro Morata is a centre-forward who has scored key goals for the Spanish national team, as well as in his club career with Real Madrid, Juventus, Chelsea, Atlético Madrid and then back on loan to Juventus. Morata played for Spain at various age-group levels before helping them to victory at the 2013 UEFA European U-21 Championship. He made his senior debut in 2014, and represented Spain at the UEFA EURO in 2016 and 2020. He scored the crucial goal that beat Sweden and sent Spain to Qatar.

RECORD AT PREVIOUS TOURNAMENTS

1930	DID NOT ENTER
1934	QUARTER-FINALS
1938	WITHDREW
1950	FOURTH PLACE
1954	DID NOT QUALIFY
1958	DID NOT QUALIFY
1962	FIRST ROUND
1966	FIRST ROUND
1970	DID NOT QUALIFY
1974	DID NOT QUALIFY
1978	FIRST ROUND
1982	SECOND ROUND
1986	QUARTER-FINALS
1990	SECOND ROUND
1994	QUARTER-FINALS
1998	FIRST ROUND
2002	QUARTER-FINALS
2006	SECOND ROUND
2010	CHAMPIONS
2014	FIRST ROUND
2018	SECOND ROUND

British workers. The national side made their debut at the 1920 Olympics and went on to reach the quarter-finals of the 1928 Olympic Games and the 1934 FIFA World Cup™, on both occasions, losing to Italy.

The Spanish Civil War and Second World War halted national-team competition for almost a decade and Spain were absent from the international headlines until they won the UEFA European Championship as hosts in 1964. A side guided by Luis Suárez, one of Spain's greatest playmakers, beat the Soviet Union 2-1 in Madrid to clinch Spain's first major trophy.

Over the next 30 years, Spain's greatest achievement was finishing as runners-up at the 1984 European Championship and reaching the World Cup quarter-finals in 1986. Finally, they achieved a title breakthrough in 1992. Gold-medal success at the Barcelona Olympics was followed by the rise of superb home-grown players from Barcelona, such as playmakers Xavi and Andrés Iniesta.

Xavi, Iniesta and other Barcelona club-mates, plus Real Madrid's goalkeeper-captain Iker Casillas and Sergio Ramos, provided the nucleus of a national team that reached historic

heights. Between November 2006 and June 2009, Spain were unbeaten for a record-equalling 35 games.

Fernando Torres scored the goal that beat Germany in the UEFA EURO final in 2008 and was one of four repeat winners in 2012. Iniesta was named best player at UEFA EURO 2012 to enhance the reputation he had established with his extra-time winner in the 2010 World Cup final victory over the Netherlands. Four years later, Spain fell in the group stage in Brazil and then in the round of 16 in Russia. *La Roja* will be determined to make amends in Qatar.

COSTA RICA

FIFA WORLD CUP
Qatar2022

Costa Rica have made five appearances at the FIFA World Cup finals and continue to dream of emulating their outstanding campaign in Brazil in 2014 when they lost only on penalties in the quarter-finals to the Netherlands.

COACH
LUIS FERNANDO SUÁREZ

ONES TO WATCH

KEYLOR NAVAS
BORN: 15 DECEMBER 1986
CLUB: PARIS SAINT-GERMAIN
(FRA)

BRYAN RUIZ
BORN: 18 AUGUST 1985
CLUB: ALAJUELENSE

Los Ticos maintained their momentum by reaching the quarter-finals and then the semi-finals of the Concacaf Gold Cup in 2015 and 2017, while qualifying again for the FIFA World Cup finals in Russia. This time their adventure ended in the first round, although later they followed up by reaching the quarter-finals of the Gold Cup in 2019 and 2021.

Simultaneously, Costa Rica were back in action in the World Cup qualifying tournament for Qatar. Their status and recent record ensured that they were among the top-five seeded teams who were placed directly in the final mini-league.

They started hesitantly with a draw in Panama and a home defeat by Mexico. This was followed by further draws against Jamaica and Honduras before Costa Rica recorded a first win in what was their fifth match by 2-1 against El Salvador. The loss of so many early points proved costly in the final standings. Costa Rica's last match was a 2-0 home win over the USA. Goals from Juan Pablo Vargas and Anthony Contreras lifted them level on points with their third-placed opponents but with an inferior goal difference. Costa Rica thus claimed fourth place and the play-off opportunity four points ahead of Panama.

Football had been introduced to Costa Rica in 1886 by a student, Óscar Pinto Fernández, who returned home from England with a ball in his luggage. A national governing body was founded in 1921. Since then, Costa Rica's national team have registered three triumphs in the Concacaf Gold Cup championship plus eight victories in the *Copa Centroamericana*. They have also twice reached the quarter-finals, as guest invitees, at the CONMEBOL *Copa América*.

ABOVE: Costa Rica missed direct qualification on goal difference.

NEW ZEALAND

New Zealand are the major soccer nation in Oceania, the only FIFA confederation without a guaranteed spot at the World Cup finals, needing an intercontinental play-off. This time around qualifying was complicated by restrictions due to the COVID-19 pandemic.

COACH
DANNY HAY

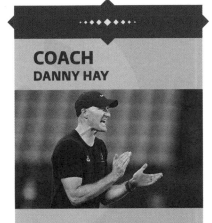

ONES TO WATCH

CHRIS WOOD
BORN: 7 DECEMBER 1991
CLUB: NEWCASTLE UNITED (ENG)

STEFAN MARINOVIC
BORN: 7 OCTOBER 1991
CLUB: HAPOEL NOF HAGALIL (ISR)

The eventual showdown was a tournament staged in Qatar in March this year. New Zealand were drawn in a four-team group and won all their three games with a 12-1 aggregate margin. Their most decisive win was by 7-1 over New Caledonia with two goals apiece from Alexander Greive and Chris Wood. Defender Liberato Cacace scored the lone goal that beat Tahiti in the semi-finals en route to a 5-1 victory over the Solomon Islands in the final.

Wood was the competition's five-goal leading scorer. The 30-year-old is New Zealand's all-time leading scorer with more than 30 goals. Wood has played all his major club career in England, including spells with West Bromwich Albion, Leicester City, Leeds United, Burnley and Newcastle United.

His team-mates, selected by coach Danny Hay, are spread all around the world. A majority are based in Europe with others in North America as well as a little nearer home from the Wellington Phoenix club who compete in the Australian A-League.

Soccer in New Zealand traces its roots back to the 1880s, with a football association formed in 1903. Their first international matches were played against Australia in 1922, though New Zealand Football did not join FIFA until 1948. It was a founder member of the Oceania confederation in 1966 after which the national team made their World Cup debut in the qualifying competition for the 1970 finals. Since then, New Zealand have appeared at the World Cup finals in 1982 and 2010, and represented Oceania four times at the FIFA Confederations Cup.

ABOVE: New Zealand were finalists previously in 1982 and 2010.

FIFA WORLD CUP
Qatar2022™

GERMANY

Germany have triumphed at the FIFA World Cup on four occasions and head to the 2022 finals in Qatar determined to improve on their results in Russia four years ago. Coach Hansi Flick has refashioned the squad since his appointment last year.

COACH
HANSI FLICK

Flick, born on 24 February 1965, succeeded Joachim Löw as coach of Germany in the summer of 2021. Previously, the former Bayern Munich midfielder had been a member of the national team's coaching staff between 2006 and the 2014 World Cup win, after which he became the German Football Association's sporting director. He returned to club football as the coach of Bayern in the autumn of 2019 and guided them to success in the UEFA Champions League, *Bundesliga*, German Cup, UEFA Super Cup and FIFA Club World Cup. Between February and September 2020, his Bayern team won a German record 23 successive matches.

Die Mannschaft's proud World Cup record also includes the status of either runners-up or third place on four occasions each. They reached the semi-finals on their World Cup debut in 1934 in Italy, then achieved a first victory in 1954 as West Germany. Renowned coach Sepp Herberger steered his outsiders to a 3-2 victory over favourites Hungary in the so-called *Wunder von Bern* ("Miracle of Bern"). Victory secured legendary status for stars such as brothers Fritz and Ottmar Walter, and goalscoring match-winner Helmut Rahn.

From then on, the German national team continued to grow in stature. They were semi-finalists in 1958, quarter-finalists in 1962 and runners-up in 1966, when a team captained by Uwe Seeler and featuring a new talent in Franz Beckenbauer lost 4-2 to hosts England after extra time.

The mid-1970s belonged to the Germans at both national-team and club level. Beckenbauer's Bayern Munich side won a hat-trick of UEFA European Cups in 1974, 1975 and 1976 and provided the nucleus of the national side that won the World Cup in 1974, as well as the UEFA European Championship in 1972 and 1980.

Beckenbauer revolutionised the sweeper's role into one of attack as well as defence, while Gerd Müller scored 68 goals in 62 international games. Later, heroes included Karl-Heinz Rummenigge, Lothar Matthäus, Rudi Völler, Jürgen Klinsmann, Thomas Häßler and Matthias Sammer.

A third World Cup success was achieved through a 1-0 victory over Argentina in Italy in 1990. Beckenbauer was now team coach and the second man, after Brazil's Mário Zagallo, to have won as both player and boss. German reunification later that year provided new resources which led to victory at UEFA EURO 1996. That was the

ABOVE: Germany last won the FIFA World Cup in 2014.

⬢ ONES TO WATCH

JOSHUA KIMMICH
BORN: 8 FEBRUARY 1995
CLUB: BAYERN MUNICH

Kimmich began his career in Stuttgart's youth team before making his name with RB Leipzig and then Bayern Munich. Initially considered a right-back, his versatility soon saw him playing in midfield. In the 2019–2020 season, he helped Bayern Munich to success in the UEFA Champions League, *Bundesliga*, German Cup and German Super Cup, followed by the FIFA Club World Cup. Kimmich made his senior national-team debut in the group stage of UEFA EURO 2016 and was named in the official UEFA Team of the Tournament.

SERGE GNABRY
BORN: 14 JULY 1995
CLUB: BAYERN MUNICH

Gnabry made a sensational impact with a hat-trick in an 8–0 win over San Marino in November 2016. Three months earlier, he had been six-goal joint top scorer as Germany claimed a silver medal at the Olympic Games. Gnabry, born in Stuttgart, played club football with Arsenal before eventually returning to Germany to play for Werder Bremen, 1899 Hoffenheim and Bayern Munich. In the 2019–2020 season, he scored 23 goals as Bayern landed the treble of the UEFA Champions League, *Bundesliga* and German Cup.

RECORD AT PREVIOUS TOURNAMENTS

1930	DID NOT ENTER
1934	THIRD PLACE
1938	FIRST ROUND
1950	DID NOT ENTER
1954	CHAMPIONS
1958	FOURTH PLACE
1962	QUARTER-FINALS
1966	RUNNERS-UP
1970	THIRD PLACE
1974	CHAMPIONS
1978	SECOND ROUND
1982	RUNNERS-UP
1986	RUNNERS-UP
1990	CHAMPIONS
1994	QUARTER-FINALS
1998	QUARTER-FINALS
2002	RUNNERS-UP
2006	THIRD PLACE
2010	THIRD PLACE
2014	CHAMPIONS
2018	GROUP STAGE

Germans' last senior title until Brazil 2014, when a strike from Mario Götze late in extra time defeated Argentina in the World Cup final at the Maracanã.

By this point, Joachim Löw had succeeded Klinsmann as coach after the third-place finish as hosts in 2006. His key men included goalkeeper Manuel Neuer, versatile Philipp Lahm, playmaker Toni Kroos and free-scoring Miroslav Klose. Löw's reign also saw Germany finish as UEFA EURO 2008 runners-up and reach two further semi-finals. He then launched Germany on the road to Qatar in the spring of 2021 before stepping down

after the UEFA EURO finals, which had been postponed by a year because of the COVID-19 pandemic.

Germany were drawn in European Group J and ended the qualifying campaign with a commanding nine-point advantage over North Macedonia. They won nine of their ten matches, scoring 36 goals and conceding only four to achieve an impressive goal difference of +32.

The journey began positively with victories over Iceland and Romania before a surprising 2-1 home defeat in Duisburg to North Macedonia. That was Löw's last World Cup

involvement. His focus then switched to the rescheduled UEFA EURO, before Flick took up the baton to revive the World Cup qualifying adventure in the autumn. Flick's team never put a foot wrong, with a succession of victories over Liechtenstein (twice), Armenia (twice), Iceland, Romania and North Macedonia. The 4-0 victory over North Macedonia saw Germany become the first nation to secure qualification, to join hosts Qatar.

Serge Gnabry, İlkay Gündoğan and Timo Werner were the group's five-goal joint top scorers. A further four goals were contributed by Leroy Sané.

JAPAN

Japan will be present at the FIFA World Cup finals for the seventh successive time. The *Blue Samurai* have yet to progress, however, beyond the round of 16. Taking that next step forward will be the focus for Hajime Moriyasu's team in Qatar.

COACH
HAJIME MORIYASU

Hajime Moriyasu, born on 23 August 1968, played 35 times in midfield for Japan between 1992 and 1996. He was one of the outstanding Japanese player pioneers in the J.League with Sanfrecce Hiroshima, Kyoto Purple Sanga and Vegalta Sendai. Moriyasu then found immediate success on being appointed coach of Sanfrecce after retirement. He guided them to a hat-trick of J.League titles between 2012 and 2015, two victories in the Japanese Super Cup and third place in the FIFA Club World Cup in 2015. Moriyasu was appointed the assistant to Akira Nishino at the 2018 World Cup and succeeded to the top job after the finals.

Football had always taken a back seat in Japan's sporting hierarchy until a national team won the bronze medal at the football tournament of the summer Olympic Games in Mexico City in 1968. That statement of potential provided the encouragement which led the association to launch an ambitious campaign to become the first Asian hosts of the World Cup.

This project included the 1993 launch of the J.League with new clubs supported by a matrix of private sponsors and local authorities. Foreign stars such as Zico of Brazil, Gary Lineker of England, Italy's Toto Schillaci and Pierre Littbarski of Germany were signed to help promote the league at home and abroad.

The immediate reward was FIFA's award to Japan of co-hosting rights with Korea Republic to the 2002 World Cup. The first staging of the finals in Asia was hailed for the excellence of its organisation while Japan, having been finalists for the first time four years earlier in France, reached the round of 16 before losing to Turkey.

Japan, with a sound professional foundation in the J.League, went from strength to strength. In the World Cup in 2006, new stars such as Hidetoshi Nakata and Junichi Inamoto shone, though Japan fell in the group stage. In 2010, a recast team reached the round of 16 on foreign soil for the first time. Japan lost only on a penalty shoot-out to Paraguay, suffered a group stage exit in 2014 and were then edged out 3-2 by powerful Belgium in the round of 16 in Russia four years ago.

No-one can doubt the power and potential of Japanese football, at the level of both country and clubs.

ABOVE: Japan are making a seventh successive appearance in the finals.

ONES TO WATCH

YUYA OSAKO
BORN: 18 MAY 1990
CLUB: VISSEL KOBE

Yuya Osako made the world sit up when he struck eight goals in two successive FIFA World Cup qualifying ties against Mongolia and Myanmar. The Vissel Kobe forward loves the big occasion. He scored in Japan's victory over Colombia in their opening match at the 2018 finals in Russia. The following year Osako scored four goals to lead Japan to the final of the AFC Asian Cup. Osako launched his professional career with Kashima Antlers in 2009 and had spells with 1860 Munich, 1FC Köln and Werder Bremen. He was Japan's 2018 Footballer of the Year.

MAYA YOSHIDA
BORN: 24 AUGUST 1988
CLUB: SAMPDORIA (ITA)

Maya Yoshida is one of Japan's most experienced defenders, with more than 110 appearances since making his debut in 2010. He also represented Japan at three Olympic Games football tournaments and captained Japan as far as the last four in both 2012 and 2021. He was an Asian Cup-winner in 2011 and was outstanding at the heart of Japan's defence in the FIFA World Cup finals in both 2014 and 2018. Yoshida began his career with Nagoya Grampus, then moved to Europe with VVV Venlo in the Netherlands, England's Southampton and Italy's Sampdoria.

RECORD AT PREVIOUS TOURNAMENTS

1930	DID NOT ENTER
1934	DID NOT ENTER
1938	WITHDREW
1950	WITHDREW
1954	DID NOT QUALIFY
1958	DID NOT ENTER
1962	DID NOT QUALIFY
1966	DID NOT ENTER
1970	DID NOT QUALIFY
1974	DID NOT QUALIFY
1978	DID NOT QUALIFY
1982	DID NOT QUALIFY
1986	DID NOT QUALIFY
1990	DID NOT QUALIFY
1994	DID NOT QUALIFY
1998	FIRST ROUND
2002	ROUND OF 16
2006	FIRST ROUND
2010	ROUND OF 16
2014	FIRST ROUND
2018	ROUND OF 16

Japan have won the AFC Asian Cup a record four times and its clubs have carried off the AFC Champions League on seven occasions.

The qualifying competition to reach the FIFA World Cup 2022 in Qatar was complicated by travel restrictions enforced by the COVID-19 pandemic.

Asia had again been granted four direct slots at the finals and the first two rounds of the qualification process also doubled up as preliminaries for the 2023 AFC Asian Cup. Japan's status in the FIFA/Coca-Cola World Ranking as of April 2019 saw them granted a bye direct to the second

round. But the initial matches had to be delayed from March and June of 2020 to early 2021. The third round was then played out between September 2021 and March 2022.

Japan were drawn in second round Group F and had no problems finishing top of the table unbeaten after winning all eight matches against Tajikistan, Kyrgyzstan, Mongolia and Myanmar. They conceded only two goals and scored 46 including victories by 14-0 against Mongolia and 10-0 against Myanmar. Yuya Osako scored a hat-trick against Mongolia and five more against Myanmar.

Despite his feats in those two matches, however, Japan's leading marksman in the group matches was Takumi Minamino with nine goals.

The third round comprised two groups of six teams and here Japan had greater difficulty before clinching the second secure qualifying slot in Group B. Despite defeats to Oman and Australia, they finished one point behind Saudi Arabia and a safe seven points clear of the third-placed *Socceroos*. Minamino and Osako, with ten goals apiece, were joint third in the overall ranking of Asian qualifying marksmen.

BELGIUM

Belgium's *Red Devils* have a proud record at the FIFA World Cup. They were fourth in Mexico in 1986 and finished third in Russia four years ago. Notably, they were also one of the four European pioneers who competed at the inaugural tournament in Uruguay.

COACH
ROBERTO MARTÍNEZ

Roberto Martínez, born on 13 July 1973, is a Spanish former midfielder who has been in charge of the Belgian national team since succeeding Marc Wilmots in August 2016. He began his playing career at Real Zaragoza, with whom he won the *Copa del Rey*, and moved to England with Wigan Athletic in 1995. Later, he played for Scotland's Motherwell, England's Walsall and then Wales's Swansea City, whose manager he became in 2007. In 2013, he guided Wigan to FA Cup victory before moving to Everton and then taking the Belgium job in 2016. He led the *Red Devils* to third place at the 2018 World Cup and to the summit of the FIFA/Coca-Cola World Ranking.

Founded in 1895, the Belgian Football Association created the second-oldest league outside Great Britain and was one of the forces behind the formation of FIFA in 1904. This pedigree led to Belgium being among the World Cup history-makers when they were eliminated in the first round after defeats by the USA and Paraguay.

Progress at international level was hampered by the amateur nature of the Belgian domestic game. Pressure for change developed in the late 1950s and 1960s along with the creation and high-speed expansion of international competitive football at both national-team and club level. Amateurism was discarded formally only in 1972 and the results were immediate.

The 1970s saw Anderlecht win the European Cup Winners' Cup twice and Club Brugge become the first Belgian side to reach the final of the European Cup (the precursor to the UEFA Champions League). The national team appeared at the World Cup on only one occasion across the 1950s, 1960s and 1970s. However, they reached the semi-finals of two out of four European Championships between 1972 and 1984, finishing as runners-up to West Germany in Italy in 1980.

An outstanding squad of players in the 1980s boasted many of Belgium's most celebrated stars, including goalkeeper Jean-Marie Pfaff, full-back Eric Gerets and 96-cap forward Jan Ceulemans. That crop's finest hour came at the 1986 World Cup, where they lost to eventual champions Argentina only in the semi-finals. Playmaker Enzo Scifo was another emergent hero.

Belgium went on to finish fourth in what proved the second of six

ABOVE: Belgium had been long-time world-ranking leaders.

ONES TO WATCH

ROMELU LUKAKU
BORN: 13 MAY 1993
CLUB: CHELSEA (ENG)

Romelu Lukaku made headlines as a teenage centre-forward for Anderlecht. He made his senior debut for the Belgian national team at the age of 17 in 2010 and is their record scorer with around 70 goals in more than 100 appearances. After leaving Anderlecht, his club career took him to Chelsea, West Bromwich Albion, Everton and Manchester United, and then to Italy. In 2020–2021, Lukaku was Inter Milan's leading marksman with 24 goals as the club won the *Serie A* title for the first time in a decade. He then returned to Chelsea for a club-record GBP 97.5m fee.

THIBAUT COURTOIS
BORN: 11 MAY 1992
CLUB: REAL MADRID (SPA)

Thibaut Courtois was awarded the adidas Golden Glove at the tournament in Russia. He was subsequently awarded The Best FIFA Men's Goalkeeper prize. Courtois was the youngest goalkeeper to make his senior debut for Belgium, winning his first cap at 19 in October 2011. He established himself as the *Red Devils*' first-choice custodian while building his club career with Genk, Atlético Madrid, Chelsea and Real Madrid. Courtois has won league titles in Belgium, Spain and England as well as the FIFA Club World Cup and the UEFA Europa League and Super Cup.

RECORD AT PREVIOUS TOURNAMENTS

1930	FIRST ROUND
1934	FIRST ROUND
1938	FIRST ROUND
1950	WITHDREW
1954	FIRST ROUND
1958	DID NOT QUALIFY
1962	DID NOT QUALIFY
1966	DID NOT QUALIFY
1970	FIRST ROUND
1974	DID NOT QUALIFY
1978	DID NOT QUALIFY
1982	SECOND ROUND
1986	FOURTH PLACE
1990	SECOND ROUND
1994	SECOND ROUND
1998	FIRST ROUND
2002	SECOND ROUND
2006	DID NOT QUALIFY
2010	DID NOT QUALIFY
2014	QUARTER-FINALS
2018	THIRD PLACE

successive appearances at the World Cup. They missed out in 2006 and 2010 but reached the quarter-finals in Brazil in 2014 with a team refashioned by coach Marc Wilmots around another outstanding generation. Wilmots stepped down after Belgium again reached the quarter-finals of the UEFA EURO in France in 2016. Successor Roberto Martínez, only Belgium's second foreign coach since the late 1950s, led them to third place in Russia and several years atop the FIFA/Coca-Cola Men's World Ranking.

World-class players such as Thibaut Courtois in goal, Kevin De Bruyne in midfield and Romelu Lukaku at centre-forward helped the *Red Devils* go undefeated en route to the World Cup in Qatar.

Belgium were drawn in European qualifying Group E. They took immediate command in March 2021 by winning 3-1 at home to Wales, drawing 1-1 away to the Czech Republic and then thrashing Belarus 8-0 back at home. The eight goals were shared among six players, with two each for Hans Vanaken and Leandro Trossard.

Belgian attention was then diverted to the UEFA EURO, where they suffered a rare defeat, going down 2-1 to eventual champions Italy in the quarter-finals in Munich. However, they were quickly back into their winning stride once the World Cup qualifiers resumed, with three victories in seven days over Estonia, the Czech Republic and Belarus again. They secured their place in Qatar with a game to spare after defeating Estonia 3-1 at the King Baudouin Stadium in Brussels. The goals were delivered by the injured Lukaku's deputy Christian Benteke in the first half and then Yannick Carrasco and Thorgan Hazard after the interval. As a satisfied Martínez said: "We did what we had to do."

CANADA

Canada are back at the FIFA World Cup finals for the second time, and after an absence of 36 years. Their domestic game has made enormous strides in part due to the popularity generated by the successful joint bid to host the 2026 finals with Mexico and the USA.

COACH
JOHN HERDMAN

John Herdman, born on 19 July 1975, is the only coach to have achieved qualifications for both the women's and men's FIFA World Cups. Herdman, from north-east England, launched himself into the world game in New Zealand 20 years ago. He took up senior development roles with New Zealand Football before leading the women's team to the FIFA Women's World Cups in 2007 and 2011. Herdman then moved to Canada and guided their women's team to a bronze medal at the Olympic Games in both 2012 and 2016. He took over the men's team in 2018 and raised them from 72nd to 33rd in the FIFA ranking on the way to Qatar.

The qualifying campaign was no simple task. Canada were not among the five top-ranked Concacaf nations seeded to the final play-off league. This meant a long and winding road to the finals. The first round involved contesting a group also featuring Suriname, Bermuda, Aruba and the Cayman Islands. They posed few problems. Canada played their four games in Florida, winning all of them by scoring 27 goals and conceding only one.

Their most decisive victory was by 11-0 against the Cayman Islands. The 11 goals were shared around seven players. Lucas Cavallini scored a hat-trick and two goals each were provided by star wing back Alphonso Davies and Mark-Anthony Kaye. Canada thus qualified for a two-leg second-round tie against Haiti. Victories by 1-0 in Port-au-Prince and 3-0 in Bridgeview, Illinois, propelled them into the all-important third round mini-league.

Three places in the finals were at stake, plus a slot in the intercontinental play-offs. The Canadians made a slow start with four draws against Honduras, the USA, Mexico and Jamaica in their opening five matches. They then hit their stride with six wins in succession. A 4-0 victory over Jamaica in Toronto secured their return to the FIFA World Cup finals with one match still to play. Canada ultimately topped the table, ahead of Mexico on goal difference and three points clear of the third-placed USA.

Cyle Larin was the group's 13-goal top scorer followed by nine-goal team-mate Jonathan David.

Football took hold in Canada at the turn of the century but struggled to establish itself in a vast country against

ABOVE: Canada will be joint hosts in 2026.

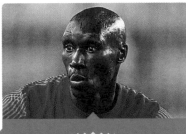

CYLE LARIN
BORN: 17 APRIL 1995
CLUB: BEŞIKTAŞ (TUR)

Cyle Larin top-scored with 13 goals in leading Canada through all three rounds of the Concacaf qualifying competition. Larin was born and brought up in Brampton, Ontario, where he played his early football with the Sigma academy. He entered Major League Soccer with Orlando City in 2015 and moved to Turkey with Beşiktaş in 2018. Larin made his senior Canada debut against Bulgaria in 2014. In the 2022 World Cup qualifying competition, his marksmanship saw him surpass Dwayne De Rosario's record of 22 goals for Canada's national team.

ATIBA HUTCHINSON
BORN: 8 FEBRUARY, 1983
CLUB: BEŞIKTAŞ (TUR)

Atiba Hutchinson is captain and record international, with a century of team appearances in sight at the end of the FIFA World Cup qualifiers. Midfielder Hutchinson turned professional in 2002 with York Region Shooters in Ontario and transferred to Toronto Lynx before heading to Östers IF of Sweden. He played in Denmark and the Netherlands before joining Beşiktaş in 2013. Hutchinson starred for Canada at youth level before making his senior debut in a friendly against the USA in 2003. He has represented Canada at six Concacaf Gold Cups.

RECORD AT PREVIOUS TOURNAMENTS

1930	DID NOT ENTER
1934	DID NOT ENTER
1938	DID NOT ENTER
1950	DID NOT ENTER
1954	DID NOT ENTER
1958	DID NOT QUALIFY
1962	DID NOT ENTER
1966	DID NOT ENTER
1970	DID NOT QUALIFY
1974	DID NOT QUALIFY
1978	DID NOT QUALIFY
1982	DID NOT QUALIFY
1986	FIRST ROUND
1990	DID NOT QUALIFY
1994	DID NOT QUALIFY
1998	DID NOT QUALIFY
2002	DID NOT QUALIFY
2006	DID NOT QUALIFY
2010	DID NOT QUALIFY
2014	DID NOT QUALIFY
2018	DID NOT QUALIFY

competition from hugely popular national sports such as ice hockey, with baseball, gridiron football and basketball crossing over from the USA. Even so, Galt from Ontario made history at the 1904 Olympic Games in St Louis. Soccer was a demonstration sport but Galt took the honours by winning what would prove Canada's only major honour for 80 years.

The national side made sporadic appearances in the 1920s but largely went into hibernation until the 1950s, when Canada made a debut in the 1958 World Cup qualifying competition. However, progress to the finals eluded them. Even when Montreal hosted the 1976 Olympic Games, Canada were eliminated in the first round of the men's football tournament.

Various attempts to launch professional soccer in north America in the late 1960s and 1970s saw three Canadian clubs, from Vancouver, Toronto and Edmonton, competing in the North American Soccer League. Toronto Metros-Croatia won the NASL Soccer Bowl in 1976, to be followed by Vancouver Whitecaps in 1979. Many of the Canadians playing in the NASL formed the backbone of the national side that won the 1985 Concacaf Championship to reach the World Cup finals for the first time in 1986.

Canada failed to progress beyond an awkward first-round group featuring the Soviet Union, France and Hungary. They came tantalisingly close to the finals again in 1994 but lost to Australia after a penalty shoot-out in an intercontinental play-off. Six years later, Canada finally recorded a second success in the Concacaf Gold Cup. Goals from Jason de Vos and Carlo Corazzin brought a 2-0 victory over guest entrants Colombia in the final in Los Angeles.

MOROCCO

Morocco are back in the FIFA World Cup finals for only the second time since 1998. The work of coach Vahid Halilhodžić over the past three years has been rewarded with an ability to score goals with fluent positive football, which augurs well for the finals.

COACH
VAHID HALILHODŽIĆ

Vahid Halilhodžić, born on 15 October 1952, played 15 times in attack for the former Yugoslavia between 1976 and 1985 while starring for Velež Mostar and then Nantes and Paris Saint-Germain in France. His coaching career took him to Morocco, France, Turkey, Saudi Arabia, Côte d'Ivoire and Croatia before he guided Algeria beyond the group stage of the FIFA World Cup for the first time in their history in 2014. Halilhodžić returned to Trabzonspor in Turkey for a second time before qualifying Japan for the finals of the 2018 FIFA World Cup. He spent a year in France with Nantes before being appointed by Morocco in 2019.

The *Atlas Lions* first appeared on the global stage at the World Cup finals in Mexico in 1970. Their second adventure was also in Mexico in 1986, when they topped a first-round group featuring England and Portugal. That achievement made Morocco only the second national team from outside Europe and the Americas to reach the second round. Here the adventure ended in a 1-0 defeat by eventual runners-up West Germany.

Three further appearances at the finals followed in 1994 and 1998 and then, after a 20-year absence, in 2018. On all three occasions, Morocco were unable to progress beyond the group stage. In Russia, an impressive 2-2 draw with Spain in their last group match was not enough to save them from an early flight home.

Morocco achieved their sixth appearance at the finals in 52 years in impressive style from first match to last.

In the second-round group stage, they won all of their six games against rivals Guinea-Bissau, Guinea and Sudan. The margin was decisive. Morocco scored 20 goals and conceded only one to open up a 12-point gap ahead of runners-up Guinea-Bissau. World Cup veteran Ayoub El Kaabi was the group's leading marksman with five goals, followed by Belgium-born team-mate Ryan Mmaee with four.

Progress secured a third-round play-off against Congo DR for the right to step out at the finals in Qatar. Congolese fans in Kinshasa were thrilled when the hosts grabbed a first-leg lead after only 12 minutes, but Morocco hit back with a late

ABOVE: Morocco qualified in decisive fashion.

⬢ ONES TO WATCH

ACHRAF HAKIMI
BORN: 4 NOVEMBER 1998
CLUB: PARIS SAINT-GERMAIN
(FRA)

Achraf Hakimi is an adventurous right wing-back. Born in Madrid, he graduated through the Real academy, spent two years on loan to Borussia Dortmund, winning the German cup, then joined Inter for EUR 40m. Hakimi helped them win Serie A and was sold to Paris Saint-Germain in 2021 for EUR 60m. Hakimi, whose family are Moroccan, played at youth level for Morocco before making his senior debut in 2016. He featured in Morocco's squad at the 2018 FIFA World Cup and the 2019 and 2021 Africa Cup of Nations.

ROMAIN SAISS
BORN: 26 MARCH, 1990
CLUB: WOLVERHAMPTON
WANDERERS (ENG)

Romain Saiss is Morocco's captain and can play in central defence or defensive midfield. He was born and brought up in south-eastern France and played lower league football with Valence, Le Havre and Clermont before making a top-tier breakthrough with Angers. In 2016 he moved to English football with Wolverhampton Wanderers for whom he has made more than 200 appearances. Saiss made his Morocco debut in 2012, and is their most experienced player after appearances at the 2018 World Cup and in three Africa Cup of Nations tournaments.

RECORD AT PREVIOUS TOURNAMENTS

1930	DID NOT EXIST
1934	DID NOT EXIST
1938	DID NOT EXIST
1950	DID NOT EXIST
1954	DID NOT EXIST
1958	DID NOT ENTER
1962	DID NOT QUALIFY
1966	WITHDREW
1970	FIRST ROUND
1974	DID NOT QUALIFY
1978	DID NOT QUALIFY
1982	DID NOT QUALIFY
1986	ROUND OF 16
1990	DID NOT QUALIFY
1994	FIRST ROUND
1998	FIRST ROUND
2002	DID NOT QUALIFY
2006	DID NOT QUALIFY
2010	DID NOT QUALIFY
2014	DID NOT QUALIFY
2018	FIRST ROUND

equaliser from Gent winger Tarik Tissoudali.

A 60,000 crowd turned out in the Mohammed V Stadium in Casablanca to cheer Morocco on to victory in the return four days later. Morocco swept forward confidently from the kick-off and were 2-0 ahead at half-time through one goal from Azzedine Ounahi and a second, seven minutes into stoppage time, from Tissaoudali. Ounahi and Achraf Hakimi added further goals in the second half before Congo claimed a late consolation. Morocco thus qualified 5-2 on aggregate.

In between the second and third rounds experienced coach Halilhodžić had also guided Morocco to the quarter-finals of the Africa Cup of Nations in Cameroon where they just missed out on progressing further, losing 2-1 after extra time to defending champions Egypt.

The Fédération Nationale du Maroc was founded after independence from France was attained in 1956. Morocco joined FIFA in 1960 and the African football confederation in 1966. Before then, however, Morocco had provided a stream of outstanding players to the French including Larbi Ben Barek, the so-called 'Black Pearl', and later the Marrakech-born Just Fontaine who scored a record 13 goals for France in the 1958 World Cup finals.

The national team have won the Africa Cup of Nations once in 1976, while club success at international level has included three victories in the CAF African Champions League by Raja Casablanca, two by neighbours Wydad and one by FAR Rabat. Wydad achieved the added bonus of reaching the FIFA Club World Cup in 2017 after a 2-1 aggregate win over Egypt's Al Ahly in the final of the most prestigious African club competition.

CROATIA

Croatia's results in international football have been remarkable, establishing an almost permanent presence in major tournaments between finishing third on their FIFA World Cup debut in 1998 and runners-up four years ago in Russia.

COACH
ZLATKO DALIĆ

Zlatko Dalić, born on 26 October 1966, is one of the longest-serving current national-team coaches. He was appointed in October 2017 in succession to Ante Čačić and led the team on its FIFA World Cup adventure in Russia only eight months later. Previously Dalić had taken charge of the U-21s between 2006 and 2011. At club level, he coached Varteks, Rijeka, Slaven Belupo and Albania's Dinamo Tirana before moving to the Middle East, where he coached Al-Faisaly and Al Hilal in Saudi Arabia, as well as Al-Ain in the United Arab Emirates. The latter won the Arabian Gulf League and Super Cup in 2015 and were AFC Champions League runners-up in 2016.

Footballers from Croatia played a major role within the former Yugoslavia national team that reached the semi-finals of the inaugural World Cup in 1930 in Uruguay. Few stars on the international stage have subsequently shone as brightly as Davor Šuker, who was the top scorer at the 1998 World Cup with six goals, while playmaker Luka Modrić was hailed as the most outstanding player at the finals in Russia.

The nucleus of the team that lost to France in the final in Moscow was still on hand to lead Croatia down the qualifying road to this year's tournament in Qatar. They had been drawn into a challenging Group H, which included Slovakia and Slovenia, plus 2018 hosts Russia.

Croatia made a disappointing start to their campaign in March 2021 by losing 1-0 in Slovenia before recovering lost ground with home victories over Cyprus and Malta. Modrić and Co then shifted focus to the UEFA EURO finals, where Croatia reached the round of 16 before losing 5-3 against Spain amid extra-time drama.

They returned to World Cup qualifying in September last year and immediately secured a goalless draw away to Russia in Moscow. That result would prove crucial. Victories followed away to Slovakia, at home to Slovenia and away to Cyprus before a difficult home clash with Slovakia in which Croatia recovered from going 1-0 and 2-1 down to rescue a draw. Victory in Malta set up a winner-takes-all showdown with Russia at the Stadion Poljud in Split.

Russia had a two-point lead, so Croatia had no alternative but to chase

ABOVE: Croatia were runners-up in Russia in 2018.

⚙ ONES TO WATCH

IVAN PERIŠIĆ
BORN: 2 FEBRUARY 1989
CLUB: INTER MILAN (ITA)

Ivan Perišić holds an honour that can never be beaten: the winger and attacking midfielder became the first Croatia player ever to score in a World Cup final, against France in 2018. He learned his trade at Hajduk Split and Sochaux, and was then league top scorer and Footballer of the Year in Belgium in 2011 with Club Brugge. He won the *Bundesliga* with Borussia Dortmund before moving to Wolfsburg and Inter. He also enjoyed a treble-winning loan spell at Bayern Munich. Perišić has scored more than 30 goals in over 110 international caps since 2011.

DEJAN LOVREN
BORN: 5 JULY 1989
CLUB: ZENIT SAINT PETERSBURG (RUS)

Dejan Lovren is one of the longest-serving Croatia internationals, having made his senior national-team debut in November 2009. Lovren, a resolute central defender, built his reputation with Dinamo Zagreb before transfers to France with Olympique Lyonnais and then the Premier League with Southampton. In 2014, he joined Liverpool, with whom he won the UEFA Champions League in 2019 and the league title a year later, before joining Zenit. Lovren played at the heart of Croatia's defence at the FIFA World Cup finals in 2014 and 2018.

RECORD AT PREVIOUS TOURNAMENTS

1930	DID NOT EXIST
1934	DID NOT EXIST
1938	DID NOT EXIST
1950	DID NOT EXIST
1954	DID NOT EXIST
1958	DID NOT EXIST
1962	DID NOT EXIST
1966	DID NOT EXIST
1970	DID NOT EXIST
1974	DID NOT EXIST
1978	DID NOT EXIST
1982	DID NOT EXIST
1986	DID NOT EXIST
1990	DID NOT EXIST
1994	UNABLE TO ENTER
1998	THIRD PLACE
2002	FIRST ROUND
2006	FIRST ROUND
2010	DID NOT QUALIFY
2014	FIRST ROUND
2018	RUNNERS–UP

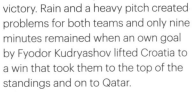

victory. Rain and a heavy pitch created problems for both teams and only nine minutes remained when an own goal by Fyodor Kudryashov lifted Croatia to a win that took them to the top of the standings and on to Qatar.

Modrić, Ivan Perišić and Mario Pašalić, with three goals each, were Croatia's joint leading scorers in the group. Modrić and Perišić had been among the stars at the World Cup finals in Russia.

Only twice have Croatia's iconic chequered red and white shirts not graced the finals of the major

international tournaments. They only missed out on the World Cup finals in 2010, and on the UEFA EURO finals in 2000. The team that reached the UEFA EURO quarter-finals at the first attempt in 1996 went on to finish third at the World Cup in France two years later.

Key players included not only centre-forward Šuker but playmakers Zvonimir Boban and Robert Prosinečki. All three had previously been FIFA World Youth Championship winners with the former Yugoslavia in 1987. Šuker scored six goals in France to win the Golden Boot. The overall outcome

of that campaign meant that Croatia had risen, in six short years, from 125th in the FIFA/Coca-Cola World Ranking to third.

Croatia failed to progress beyond the first round of the finals in 2002, 2006 and 2014, but then surged magnificently through to the final itself in Russia. They won all three group matches before defeating Denmark and Russia, both on penalties, and England in extra time, on their exciting but strength-sapping path to the final, where they were ultimately defeated by France at the Luzhniki Stadium.

BRAZIL

Brazil boast the proud record of having won the FIFA World Cup an unequalled five times. Their last triumph came in 2002, in Japan and South Korea. Regaining their crown would be a perfect way to mark the 20th anniversary of their achievement in Yokohama.

COACH
TITE

Tite (full name Adenor Leonardo Bacchi), born on 25 May 1961, was appointed in June 2016, taking the reins from former World Cup-winning captain Dunga. During his playing career, he spent 11 years as a defensive midfielder with hometown Caxias, Esportivo, Portuguesa (São Paulo) and Guarani of Campinas. He began his coaching career with the Garibaldi outfit Guarany and has managed a host of clubs in his native Brazil, as well as having had a couple of short stints abroad with Al-Ain and Al-Wahda in Abu Dhabi. His club achievements include guiding Corinthians to success in the FIFA Club World Cup™, the CONMEBOL *Libertadores* and the Brazilian top flight, and he led his country to CONMEBOL *Copa América* glory in 2019.

In addition to a run of success on the global stage kicked off in 1958, Brazil have also finished runners-up twice and are the only nation to have been ever-present at the tournament since the inaugural instalment in Uruguay in 1930. They have also played host on two occasions.

Beyond the statistics, Brazil have long entranced fans around the world thanks to the flair and explosive technical brilliance of legendary players such as Pelé, Garrincha, Didi, Romário, Bebeto, Ronaldo and Ronaldinho, giving rise to the term *jogo bonito* (beautiful game).

Their latest superstar is Neymar, who made his World Cup debut on home soil in 2014, cemented his reputation with the penalty that won Olympic gold for Brazil in Rio de Janeiro in 2016 and then became the most expensive player in football with his EUR 220m transfer to French club Paris Saint-Germain.

Brazilian football developed at the end of the 19th century, prompted by migrant British workers, with leagues established in Rio and São Paulo by the turn of the century. The national team entered the competitive arena at the South American Championship (as the CONMEBOL *Copa América* was formerly known) in 1916. They participated in the 1930 and 1934 World Cups, failing to advance on both occasions, but then reached the semi-finals in France in 1938 before losing to champions Italy.

A golden age followed between 1950 and 1970. Brazil, as hosts, were World Cup runners-up to Uruguay in 1950, reached the quarter-finals in 1954 and then won the title for the first time in Sweden in 1958. A forward line featuring Garrincha, Vavá,

ABOVE: Brazil have a proud FIFA World Cup record to defend.

⬖ ONES TO WATCH

GABRIEL JESUS
BORN: 3 APRIL 1997
CLUB: MANCHESTER CITY (ENG)

Gabriel Jesus burst onto the scene in the Brazilian domestic game in 2015. In 2016, he helped Brazil win Olympic gold for the first time, as well as leading Palmeiras to a first top-flight league title in 22 years. January 2017 saw Jesus join Manchester City, with whom he won the English Premier League title on multiple occasions, the League Cup in 2018, 2020 and 2021 as well as the FA Cup in 2019. His personal run of success also includes Brazil's victory in the CONMEBOL *Copa América* in 2019 as hosts, where he scored in the 3-1 defeat of Peru in the final.

THIAGO SILVA
BORN: 22 SEPTEMBER 1984
CLUB: CHELSEA (ENG)

Defender Thiago Emiliano da Silva's career has yielded more than 20 major national and international trophies, plus the captaincy of Brazil. Born in Rio de Janeiro, he began his career at Fluminense, which he finally left in 2009, having previously cut his teeth in Europe in 2004–2005. He then spent three seasons with AC Milan and eight with Paris Saint-Germain before joining Chelsea in 2020. He won the first of more than 100 caps in 2008 and helped Brazil to victory in the FIFA Confederations Cup in 2013, as well as the CONMEBOL *Copa América* in 2019.

RECORD AT PREVIOUS TOURNAMENTS

1930	FIRST ROUND
1934	FIRST ROUND
1938	THIRD PLACE
1950	RUNNERS-UP
1954	QUARTER-FINALS
1958	CHAMPIONS
1962	CHAMPIONS
1966	FIRST ROUND
1970	CHAMPIONS
1974	FOURTH PLACE
1978	THIRD PLACE
1982	SECOND ROUND
1986	QUARTER-FINALS
1990	SECOND ROUND
1994	CHAMPIONS
1998	RUNNERS-UP
2002	CHAMPIONS
2006	QUARTER-FINALS
2010	QUARTER-FINALS
2014	FOURTH PLACE
2018	QUARTER-FINALS

Mário Zagallo and the 17-year-old Pelé recorded a 5-2 win over their hosts in the final. In Chile in 1962, an almost identical team, minus the injured Pelé, beat Czechoslovakia 3-1 to seal glory.

The *Seleção* clinched a hat-trick in Mexico in 1970. The brilliance of Pelé, supported by the likes of Tostão, Gérson, Jairzinho and Carlos Alberto, earned Brazil the right to keep the Jules Rimet Trophy in perpetuity (although the cup was eventually stolen). Further success was attained in 1994, against Italy in Pasadena, in what was the first World Cup final settled through a penalty shoot-out.

Victory number five, against Germany, was inspired by Ronaldo in Japan and Korea Republic in 2002.

Since then, a sixth crown has proven elusive. The quarter-finals were the end of the road in 2006, in 2010 and in 2018. A CONMEBOL *Copa América* victory in 2019 was the springboard for a complex World Cup qualifying campaign. The COVID-19 pandemic forced the repeated postponement of matches, but coach Tite guided his team to the finals in Qatar with six matches to spare after a 1-0 win over Colombia in São Paulo. Midfielder Lucas Paquetá

scored the all-important goal after 72 minutes.

Along the way, Brazil had also finished runners-up in the 2021 CONMEBOL *Copa América*, while the U-23s captured a second successive Olympic gold medal.

The squad that Tite constructed on the road to Qatar was packed full of stars from European clubs. These included goalkeeper Alisson, defenders Thiago Silva, Marquinhos and Alex Sandro, midfielders Casemiro, Philippe Coutinho and Fabinho, plus forwards Gabriel Jesus, Roberto Firmino and Neymar.

SERBIA

Serbia have built a reputation as major players in international football. The natural talent of the country's footballers has long been admired and has been reflected in Serbia's presence at the FIFA World Cup finals in 2006, 2010 and 2018.

COACH
DRAGAN STOJKOVIĆ

Dragan Stojković, born on 3 March 1965, was appointed as the new national-team coach of Serbia on his birthday in March 2021, shortly before the start of the World Cup qualifying competition. "Piksi" Stojković, nicknamed after a cartoon character, has done it all. He scored 15 goals in 84 appearances for the former Yugoslavia, many of them as their captain. He was later President of the national football association and then of his old club, Red Star Belgrade, before working as a club coach in Japan and China. The national team is his first senior coaching appointment back home, succeeding Ljubiša Tumbaković.

Serbia finished third in their group at Russia 2018 and are determined to progress to the knockout stages in Qatar. They underlined their ability and threat to the established World Cup powers by finishing ahead of Cristiano Ronaldo's Portugal in European qualifying Group A.

The image of Yugoslavia as the "Argentina of Europe" was first fostered back in 1930, when they were one of only four European nations to brave the Atlantic crossing to attend the inaugural World Cup finals in Uruguay.

Player exports back then included inside forward Ivan Bek, who played for Sète in France. Bek scored one goal in a 2-1 defeat of Brazil, which put Yugoslavia in the semi-finals. Other key players included forwards Aleksandar Tirnanić and Branislav Sekulić, both of whom were later national-team managers.

Yugoslavia returned to the finals without success in 1950, despite having a squad full of future managerial talent, including Ivica Horvat, Zlatko Čajkovski, Bernard Vukas, Stjepan Bobek and Rajko Mitić. Beaten in the quarter-finals by West Germany in both 1954 and 1958, they achieved their best finish in 1962, when they finished fourth in Chile.

Yugoslavia were the runners-up in the first UEFA European Championship in 1960 and then again in 1968. Red Star Belgrade, one of their two leading clubs along with Partizan Belgrade, won the European Champions Cup and were the runners-up in the 1979 UEFA Cup before the break-up of Yugoslavia in the 1990s. Initially, the national team of a newly independent Serbia and Montenegro reached the World Cup finals in France in 1998. New heroes such as Dejan Savićević,

ABOVE: Serbia topped their European qualifying group.

ONES TO WATCH

DUŠAN VLAHOVIĆ
BORN: 28 JANUARY 2000
CLUB: FIORENTINA (ITA)

Dušan Vlahović enjoyed an explosive year in 2021, scoring 33 goals in the calendar year to equal the record for *Serie A* set by Cristiano Ronaldo in 2020. In addition, Vlahović contributed four goals to Serbia's successful World Cup qualifying campaign. He had scored in all the age-group levels before making his senior debut in a UEFA Nations League game against Hungary in October 2020. Vlahović launched his career with Partizan and set a record at 16 as their youngest debutant. He was sold to Fiorentina in 2018 when still only 18.

ALEKSANDAR MITROVIĆ
BORN: 16 SEPTEMBER 1994
CLUB: FULHAM (ENG)

Aleksandar Mitrović is Serbia's all-time top scorer but it was goal no. 44 that defeated Portugal to secure Serbia's place in Qatar. He began his career with Partizan and then played for Anderlecht before moving to Newcastle United in 2015 and Fulham three years later. Mitrović made his national-team debut in 2013, and was the tournament's Golden Player when Serbia won the European U-19 title. He played in all three matches at the 2018 FIFA World Cup finals and was their eight-goal top scorer in the qualifying campaign for Qatar.

RECORD AT PREVIOUS TOURNAMENTS

1930	FOURTH PLACE
1934	DID NOT QUALIFY
1938	DID NOT QUALIFY
1950	FIRST ROUND
1954	QUARTER-FINALS
1958	QUARTER-FINALS
1962	FOURTH PLACE
1966	DID NOT QUALIFY
1970	DID NOT QUALIFY
1974	SECOND ROUND
1978	DID NOT QUALIFY
1982	FIRST ROUND
1986	DID NOT QUALIFY
1990	QUARTER-FINALS
1994	SUSPENDED
1998	SECOND ROUND
2002	DID NOT QUALIFY
2006	FIRST ROUND
2010	FIRST ROUND
2014	DID NOT QUALIFY
2018	FIRST ROUND

Predrag Mijatović and Siniša Mihajlović led them into the second round.

Montenegro achieved independence in May 2006 and, as Serbia and Montenegro, they attended the finals of the World Cup the following month. Serbia reached the finals again in 2010, although they failed to progress beyond the group stage. They missed out in 2014, then exited at the group stage in Russia. Now they return to the finals after topping European qualifying Group A.

Serbia ended the campaign in triumph after winning the group in the most dramatic manner possible in the closing minutes of their last match away to 2016 European champions Portugal in Lisbon.

The first duel between the rivals had ended in a 2-2 draw in Belgrade in the early qualifying skirmishes back in March 2021. Even then, Serbia had to recover from two goals down. The teams kicked off the decider level on points, but a repeat draw would have sent Portugal to the finals because of a better goal difference. Only victory would be sufficient for Serbia against opponents they had never beaten.

Serbia's task grew even more challenging after only two minutes when they fell behind to a goal from Renato Sanches. However, Dušan Tadić not only equalised in the 33rd minute to keep Serb hopes alive, but also provided the cross from which substitute Aleksandar Mitrović headed a 90th-minute winner. Mitrović said, "The cross was perfect. We know each other so well. He knows where I am going to be and I know where he will put the ball."

The Serbs therefore finished unbeaten in all of their eight games and three points ahead of Portugal. Mitrović was European Group A's eight-goal leading scorer, supported by Dušan Vlahović with four goals.

SWITZERLAND

Switzerland have never won a major international tournament, but their consistency has been impressive, having competed at the FIFA World Cup finals on 11 occasions and at the UEFA EURO finals five times. This is their fifth successive appearance on the World Cup stage.

COACH
MURAT YAKIN

Murat Yakin, born on 15 September 1974, took over the national team midway through the FIFA World Cup qualifying campaign following the departure of Vladimir Petković after the UEFA EURO 2020 finals. Yakin, born in Basel, played 49 times in central defence for Switzerland. Younger brother Hakan Yakin was also a Switzerland international. His club career took him to Grasshoppers, VfB Stuttgart, Fenerbahçe and Kaiserslautern before he retired in 2006 after five years back at Basel. Yakin's club coaching career has been undertaken entirely in Switzerland, apart from a year in Russia with Spartak Moscow.

Despite the lack of senior trophies, the Swiss have always held a particular place at the forefront of international football because FIFA and Europe's governing body UEFA have their headquarters in Zurich and Nyon respectively. However, the history of the game in Switzerland stretches back to the 1880s, when the British helped develop the game as evidenced in the names of major clubs such as Grasshopper Club Zurich.

The *Nati* were runners-up at the 1924 Olympic Games and then quarter-finalists at both the 1934 and 1938 World Cups. Stars from that era included the Abegglen brothers, Max and André, who scored more than 60 international goals between them in the 1930s.

The man most responsible behind the scenes for that success was Karl Rappan, the father of Swiss football. Rappan was a former Austria international who had moved in 1931 to Switzerland, where he was successively a player and then successful coach of Geneva-based club, Servette. A deep thinker about the game, Rappan devised the *verrou* or "Swiss bolt" system. This involved using a free defender at the back, a precursor to the Italian-style *libero*.

Rappan was heavily involved in the Swiss reaching four of the five World Cups played after the war. Their best performance was in 1954 when, as hosts, they reached the quarter-finals before losing a tumultuous match 7-5 to Austria.

After 1966, the national side suffered a reversal of fortune and failed to qualify for six consecutive World Cup finals and seven UEFA EURO finals. A revival was launched under English coach Roy Hodgson.

ABOVE: Switzerland qualified with a dramatic last-match victory.

⬟ ONES TO WATCH

YANN SOMMER

BORN: 17 DECEMBER 1988
CLUB: BORUSSIA
MÖNCHENGLADBACH (GER)

Yann Sommer is one of football's finest goalkeepers, after his performances at the last FIFA World Cup and UEFA EURO. He began his career at Basel and impressed in loan spells with Vaduz and Grasshoppers. Sommer returned to Basel to win the Swiss league title four times and the cup once. Since 2014, he has played for Borussia Mönchengladbach. He represented Switzerland at U-16, U-17, U-19 and U-21 levels before making his senior national debut against Romania in a friendly in 2012.

XHERDAN SHAQIRI

BORN: 10 OCTOBER 1991
CLUB: CHICAGO FIRE (USA)

Xherdan Shaqiri celebrated his 100th senior international cap with a 4-0 victory over Bulgaria in November 2021 that propelled the team to the FIFA World Cup finals. He made his Switzerland debut against Uruguay in March 2010. Shaqiri was born in the dissolving Yugoslavia to Kosovar Albanian parents, who emigrated to Switzerland in 1992. He won three Swiss league titles with Basel before playing for Bayern Munich, Inter and Stoke City. Next came three years at Liverpool, helping them win the UEFA Champions League, FIFA Club World Cup and Premier League.

RECORD AT PREVIOUS TOURNAMENTS

1930	DID NOT ENTER
1934	QUARTER-FINALS
1938	QUARTER-FINALS
1950	FIRST ROUND
1954	QUARTER-FINALS
1958	DID NOT QUALIFY
1962	FIRST ROUND
1966	FIRST ROUND
1970	DID NOT QUALIFY
1974	DID NOT QUALIFY
1978	DID NOT QUALIFY
1982	DID NOT QUALIFY
1986	DID NOT QUALIFY
1990	DID NOT QUALIFY
1994	SECOND ROUND
1998	DID NOT QUALIFY
2002	DID NOT QUALIFY
2006	SECOND ROUND
2010	FIRST ROUND
2014	SECOND ROUND
2018	SECOND ROUND

Switzerland narrowly missed out on qualifying for the 1992 European Championship finals, but claimed a place at the 1994 FIFA World Cup in the USA. They continued to make progress and returned to the UEFA EURO two years later. They were also EURO co-hosts with Austria in 2008.

The World Cup welcomed Switzerland back to the finals in 2006 and they have been ever-present since. In both 2006 and 2014, the Swiss reached the round of 16. Their first appearance for 67 years in the quarter-finals of a major tournament was at UEFA EURO 2020 last year,

when they lost to Spain in a penalty shoot-out. Vladimir Petković, who had been national-team coach for seven years, then returned to club football with Bordeaux in France.

His successor, Murat Yakin, was then tasked with the challenge of picking up the managerial reins in the middle of the FIFA World Cup qualifying campaign. He did so in Group C, in which original favourites Italy impressively won UEFA EURO 2020 in between World Cup action.

Switzerland had opened their campaign in March 2021 under Petković with victories away to Bulgaria

and at home to Lithuania. They resumed under Yakin in the autumn with goalless draws at home to Italy and away to Northern Ireland, but a 1-1 stalemate against Italy in Rome kept their hopes alive as they approached the last matchday. The Swiss and Italians were level on points and so the *Azzurri*'s failure to win in Northern Ireland meant Switzerland's 4-0 victory over Bulgaria fired them into the finals.

Along with Spain, Switzerland were 15-goal joint-lowest scorers among the European group winners. Breel Embolo, with three goals, was the team's leading scorer.

CAMEROON

Cameroon have been ground-breakers for African football at the FIFA World Cup. In Italy in 1990 they became the first African side to reach the quarter-finals. Now they are back, for the eighth time in all, after missing out on the finals in Russia in 2018.

COACH
RIGOBERT SONG

Rigobert Song, born on 1 July 1976, is a former defender who was appointed on 28 February 2022 to succeed Toni Conceicao for the decisive qualifying ties against Algeria. Song had previously managed the Cameroon A team and the U-23s. He totalled 137 appearances in defence for Cameroon between 1993 and 2010, appearing at four World Cup finals tournaments. He was also twice a winner in the Africa Cup of Nations. Song's club career took him to France with Metz and Lens, Italy with Salernitana, England with Liverpool and West Ham, Germany with 1FC Köln and Turkey with Galatasaray and Trabzonspor.

The story of Cameroon is one of the great success stories of African football. Cameroon had become the second of France's colonies in Sub-Saharan Africa to become independent only in 1960. The football association had been founded a year earlier in readiness and wasted no time joining the international family. Cameroon became a member of CAF in 1963 and then world governing body FIFA the following year.

The *Indomitable Lions* made their debut in the FIFA World Cup without success in the 1970 qualifiers, but that same year marked their first appearance in the Africa Cup of Nations by reaching the group stage in Sudan.

Soon they were a force with which to be reckoned. Cameroon were third in the Africa Cup of Nations in 1972, before reaching the World Cup finals for the first time in Spain in 1982. They made an instant impression. In the group stage, they marked their arrival by drawing with eventual champions Italy, Poland and Peru, but missed out on a place in the second round only on goal difference. One goal was all that separated them from the *Azzurri*.

Two years later, Cameroon achieved the first of their five successes at the Africa Cup of Nations. They were runners-up in 1986 and winners again in 1988, before making more World Cup headlines in Italy in 1990.

The *Indomitable Lions* beat reigning champions Argentina in the opening match before reaching the quarter-finals, where they lost in extra time to England. Their hero was veteran centre-forward Roger Milla. He ended the tournament as joint third-top scorer with four goals. African football in general had Cameroon's

ABOVE: Cameroon were the first African quarter-finalists in 1990.

✳ ONES TO WATCH

KARL TOKO EKAMBI
BORN: 14 SEPTEMBER, 1992
CLUB: LYON (FRA)

Karl Toko Ekambi was born in Paris. He began his career with Paris and Sochaux before transferring up to Angers. In 2018, he became the first Cameroon player to win the Prix Marc-Vivien Foé for best African player in the French league. The award was named after Marc-Vivien Foé, who died playing for Cameroon in 2003. Ekambi spent time in Spain with Villarreal before returning to French football with Lyon, initally on loan, in 2020. He was the hero of Cameroon's FIFA World Cup qualifying campaign with crucial goals against both Côte d'Ivoire and then Algeria.

MICHAEL NGADEU-NGADJUI
BORN: 23 NOVEMBER 1990
CLUB: GENT (BEL)

Michael Ngadeu-Ngadjui captained Cameroon to their FIFA World Cup qualifying success. Ngadeu was born in Cameroon and left for Europe to study engineering in Germany. While there, he played for Sandhausen and 1FC Nürnberg before turning football into a career. He played in Romania and the Czech Republic before moving to Gent. Ngadeu has anchored Cameroon's defence more than 60 times since making his national-team debut in the victorious 2017 Africa Cup of Nations campaign. He was appointed captain in 2019.

RECORD AT PREVIOUS TOURNAMENTS

1930	DID NOT EXIST
1934	DID NOT EXIST
1938	DID NOT EXIST
1950	DID NOT EXIST
1954	DID NOT EXIST
1958	DID NOT EXIST
1962	DID NOT ENTER
1966	WITHDREW
1970	DID NOT QUALIFY
1974	DID NOT QUALIFY
1978	DID NOT QUALIFY
1982	FIRST ROUND
1986	DID NOT QUALIFY
1990	QUARTER-FINALS
1994	FIRST ROUND
1998	FIRST ROUND
2002	FIRST ROUND
2006	DID NOT QUALIFY
2010	FIRST ROUND
2014	FIRST ROUND
2018	DID NOT QUALIFY

brilliant campaign to thank for helping persuade FIFA to grant the continent a third berth at the 1994 finals. Cameroon capitalised by becoming an almost permanent presence at the finals. Since their outstanding campaign in 1990, they have failed to qualify in only 2006 and 2018.

A new hero was goalscoring centre-forward Samuel Eto'o, who remains the 18-goal leading scorer in Africa Cup of Nations history. Eto'o shot to fame when Cameroon won gold at the Sydney 2000 Olympic Games football tournament. Later, he won the European Champions League

Cup twice with Barcelona and once with Internazionale. He was voted four times as African Player of the Year, an award also claimed down the years by Milla twice, Theophile Abega, Thomas N'Kono, Jean Manga Onguéné and Patrick Mboma.

The finals preceded the third and final round of the African qualifying competition for the FIFA World Cup. Cameroon topped their second-round group. They edged ahead of Côte d'Ivoire by defeating them 1-0 on the last matchday with a first-half strike from Toko Ekambi. The Lyon forward's goal qualified

Cameroon for a dramatic showdown, played home and away, against Algeria for a place in the finals in Qatar.

Cameroon were in trouble after losing 1-0 at home but recovered remarkably in Blida. Jean-Eric Choupo-Moting levelled on aggregate to send the tie into extra time. Algeria thought they had won when Ahmed Touba equalised on the night with only two minutes remaining, but Cameroon responded with an Ekambi strike that came as late as the fourth minute of stoppage time. Thus, they qualified on the away-goals rule.

PORTUGAL

Portugal had a complicated journey to their sixth successive FIFA World Cup finals, but their all-round creative and attacking talents will make them contenders in Qatar. Their ambition will be to exceed the fourth-places finishes of 1966 and 2006.

COACH
FERNANDO SANTOS

Fernando Santos, born on 10 October 1954, knows all about international football success. He steered Portugal to victory in UEFA EURO 2016. Santos had never played high-level football but proved outstanding as a club coach with Porto, AEK, Panathinaikos and PAOK in Greece, as well as with Lisbon rivals Sporting and Benfica. In 2010, he turned to national-team football with Greece. He led them to the quarter-finals of UEFA Euro 2014 and then to the second round of the 2014 FIFA World Cup. He succeeded Paulo Bento as the coach of Portugal and led them to glory in France and then the round of 16 at both the 2018 FIFA World Cup and UEFA EURO 2020.

The Portuguese Football Association was founded in 1914 by a merger of the associations of Lisbon and Oporto. The first statements at international level were made by record league title winners Benfica in winning the UEFA European Champions Cup twice (1961 and 1962) and reaching three more finals.

Benfica also provided the bulk of the national team, who finished third at the 1966 FIFA World Cup in England. Their hero was Mozambique-born striker Eusébio, Portugal's greatest player until the advent of Cristiano Ronaldo, who was the finals' nine-goal leading scorer. Playmaker Mario Coluna, also from Mozambique, was another product of the then Portuguese colony in a side that included Benfica wingers José Augusto and Antonio Simões and centre-forward José Torres.

After a "lost decade" in the 1970s, the reputation of Portuguese football was revived in the 1980s by Porto's victory in the UEFA Champions Cup and Benfica's progress to the finals of both the Champions Cup and UEFA Cup. Portugal's talented youngsters won two FIFA age-group crowns in 1989 and 1991. Star graduate Luís Figo would later be crowned both World and European Player of the Year.

Porto, under José Mourinho, won the UEFA Cup and Champions League in 2003 and 2004 to spark a further renewal of confidence. The national team profited by finishing runners-up as hosts at UEFA EURO 2004 and then took fourth place at the 2006 FIFA World Cup. This was the first World Cup graced by a young Ronaldo, who subsequently grew up into one of the game's greatest players. He holds the Portugal records for national-team

ABOVE: Portugal qualified via the European playoffs.

⬡ ONES TO WATCH

BRUNO FERNANDES
BORN: 8 SEPTEMBER 1994
CLUB: MANCHESTER UNITED
(ENG)

Bruno Fernandes was born in Portugal but launched his career with five seasons at Sampdoria. He then returned home to win domestic cup and individual awards with Sporting. Fernandes's ability to both create and score goals earned him a EUR 55m transfer in January 2020 to Manchester United, where he proved an instant success. Fernandes played for Portugal at the 2016 Olympic Games in Rio de Janeiro, made his senior international debut a year later and was a member of the 2019 UEFA Nations League winning team.

PEPE (Kepler Laveran de Lima Ferreira)
BORN: 26 FEBRUARY 1983
CLUB: PORTO

Pepe is a strong defender at club level and for his adopted country of Portugal. Born in Brazil, he moved to Portuguese football at 18. His rock-like tackling at centre-back or defensive midfield has been a feature of Portugal's appearances at three FIFA World Cups and four UEFA European Championships. He won UEFA EURO 2016 and the UEFA Nations League in 2019, while international club honours have included a FIFA Club World Cup plus a UEFA Champions League and UEFA Super Cup with Real Madrid.

RECORD AT PREVIOUS TOURNAMENTS

1930	DID NOT ENTER
1934	DID NOT QUALIFY
1938	DID NOT QUALIFY
1950	DID NOT QUALIFY
1954	DID NOT QUALIFY
1958	DID NOT QUALIFY
1962	DID NOT QUALIFY
1966	THIRD PLACE
1970	DID NOT QUALIFY
1974	DID NOT QUALIFY
1978	DID NOT QUALIFY
1982	DID NOT QUALIFY
1986	ROUND OF 16
1990	DID NOT QUALIFY
1994	DID NOT QUALIFY
1998	DID NOT QUALIFY
2002	FIRST ROUND
2006	FOURTH PLACE
2010	ROUND OF 16
2014	FIRST ROUND
2018	ROUND OF 16

appearances and goals and captained them to success at the UEFA EURO in 2016.

Portugal's international campaigns were then brought to a halt in the round of 16 at both the 2018 FIFA World Cup and the rescheduled UEFA EURO 2020 last year. However, in between, they did win the 2019 UEFA Nations League.

Fernando Santos approached the qualifying campaign to reach Qatar with a settled squad. In addition to the experience of "old hands" such as Ronaldo in attack, Pepe in defence plus midfielders João Moutinho and Bruno Fernandes, Portugal also benefited

from the emergence of Bernardo Silva, Diogo Jota and João Félix.

Goalkeeper Rui Patricio, Pepe, Moutinho and Ronaldo are among the exclusive band of international footballers who can boast the proud achievement of having celebrated more than 100 appearances for their national team.

Portugal opened with a 1-0 victory over Azerbaijan, folllowed by an important 2-2 draw away to Serbia, potentially their most dangerous rivals. They remained unbeaten until the crucial final qualifying tie at home to Serbia in Porto. Portugal needed

only a draw to secure their place in Qatar and were well on course after taking the lead in only the second minute through Renato Sanches. They remained notionally top of the group even after Serbia equalised, but conceding a last-minute goal meant a 2-1 defeat, a slip to second place in the table and the challenge of the play-offs.

Here, they reasserted themselves with victories over Turkey and an Italy-defeating North Macedonia side. A 2-0 victory sent Portugal to Qatar, courtesy of two goals from Bruno Fernandes. Ronaldo was Portugal's six-goal overall leading scorer.

GHANA

Ghana are four-time winners of the Africa Cup of Nations and finalists at the FIFA World Cup on three occasions. Their best performance was reaching the quarter-finals in South Africa in 2010, and they are returning in Qatar after missing out on Russia in 2018.

COACH
OTTO ADDO

Otto Addo, born on 9 June 1975 in Hamburg, Germany, was appointed the interim head coach of Ghana just before the decisive FIFA World Cup qualifying victory with Nigeria. He had previously been assistant to Milovan Rajevac, who left his post after Ghana's group-stage exit at the Africa Cup of Nations in Cameroon. Addo spent all his playing career in Germany with Hamburg, Hannover, Borussia Dortmund and Mainz. He then worked on the coaching staff of Dortmund in between taking on various roles ranging from scout to caretaker manager with the Ghana FA.

Ghana, formerly the Gold Coast, achieved independence in 1957 and their *Black Stars* national team quickly established themselves as a powerful force in African football. They won the Africa Cup of Nations in 1963, at their first attempt, and retained the trophy two years later. In the following two events, they were beaten finalists and triumphed again in 1978 and 1982. Ghana were the first nation to win the trophy four times.

In club football, Asante Kotoko have won the African Champions Cup twice and Ghana have produced many outstanding players. Mohamed Ahmed Polo and Adolf Armah were stars in the 1970s; Ibrahim Sunday, African footballer of the year in 1971, was a pioneer in Germany with Werder Bremen; Abedi Pele won many French trophies with Marseille in the

1980s; and Nii Lamptey, then of PSV Eindhoven, led Ghana to victory in the 1991 FIFA World Youth Championship.

At that point, however, Ghana were still waiting to qualify for the FIFA World Cup finals. All this changed in 2006, when Ghana qualified to play in Germany. They were there to compete, not merely make up the numbers or savour a first appearance in the World Cup spotlight.

A team starring versatile Asamoah Gyan, captain Stephen Appiah and midfielder Sulley Muntari lost their opening tie 2-0 to eventual champions Italy, but a historic first victory at the finals was achieved by 2-0 over the Czech Republic. A 2-1 defeat of the USA secured a runners-up place in the table and entry to the round of 16. Here the adventure ended in a 3-0 defeat by reigning champions Brazil. Ghana were

ABOVE: Ghana are a pioneering power in African football.

⬟ ONES TO WATCH

THOMAS PARTEY
BORN: 13 JUNE 1993
CLUB: ARSENAL (ENG)

Midfielder Thomas Partey grew up in eastern Ghana and was scouted for Spanish club Leganés at 19. He soon moved to Atlético Madrid, with whom he won the UEFA Europa League, UEFA Super Cup and Spanish league, before being sold to Arsenal in the English Premier League in 2020 for a Ghanaian record of EUR 50m. Partey, who was voted Ghana's player of the year in 2018 and 2019, made his senior national team debut in an Africa Cup of Nations tie in 2017. He was Ghana's vice-captain for last year's Cup of Nations, as well as the World Cup qualifying campaign.

JORDAN AYEW
BORN: 11 SEPTEMBER 1991
CLUB: CRYSTAL PALACE (ENG)

Jordan Ayew is a son of Ghana star Abedi Pele and a brother of internationals André and Ibrahim Ayew. Jordan was born in Marseille, for whom he made more than 100 appearances between 2009 and 2014. He also played for Sochaux on loan, and Lorient, before moving to England in 2015 with Aston Villa, then Swansea City and Crystal Palace. He emulated his father and brothers by making his Ghana debut against Swaziland in an Africa Cup of Nations tie in 2010. He played at the finals of the 2014 FIFA World Cup, as well as the 2015 Africa Cup of Nations.

RECORD AT PREVIOUS TOURNAMENTS

1930	DID NOT EXIST
1934	DID NOT EXIST
1938	DID NOT EXIST
1950	DID NOT EXIST
1954	DID NOT EXIST
1958	DID NOT EXIST
1962	DID NOT QUALIFY
1966	WITHDREW
1970	DID NOT QUALIFY
1974	DID NOT QUALIFY
1978	DID NOT QUALIFY
1982	WITHDREW
1986	DID NOT QUALIFY
1990	DID NOT QUALIFY
1994	DID NOT QUALIFY
1998	DID NOT QUALIFY
2002	DID NOT QUALIFY
2006	ROUND OF 16
2010	QUARTER–FINALS
2014	FIRST ROUND
2018	DID NOT QUALIFY

victims of Ronaldo Nazário's record 15th World Cup goal.

Ghana's headline-making campaign was the springboard to their status among the most consistent of African teams. Following the 2006 World Cup, Ghana reached the semi-finals of the Africa Cup of Nations in six successive campaigns, including a runners-up finish in 2015. Along the way, they achieved their finest World Cup performance in South Africa in 2010. Ghana came within a penalty shoot-out of reaching the semi-finals before losing in dramatic fashion to Uruguay.

The most recent Africa Cup of Nations saw Ghana register their 100th match at the finals. The campaign split a busy six months in which Ghana launched their FIFA World Cup 2022 campaign in September 2021 and then celebrated qualification for Qatar in March.

Ghana began in a second-round group, which featured challenging opposition in South Africa as well as Ethiopia and Zimbabwe. Only the group winners could progress and Ghana approached their last match hosting a South African team who were three points clear. A first-half

penalty converted by André Ayew provided Ghana with a 1-0 victory, which lifted them level on points with South Africa and above them by the slimmest possible single-goal superior goal difference. Ayew was the group's three-goal top scorer.

Ghana exited the Africa Cup of Nations at the group stage and then regrouped to take on Nigeria in the World Cup qualifying deciders. The first leg at home ended in a goalless draw, but a superb display away in Abuja ended in a 1-1 draw – a first-half goal from Thomas Partey sent Ghana to Qatar on the away-goals rule.

URUGUAY

Legendary Garra Charrua eventually fired Uruguay to Qatar. And the *Celeste* and the Qataris share a slice of World Cup history by making their debut without ever having appeared in the finals before. In Uruguay's case, in 1930, they also went on to win.

COACH
DIEGO ALONSO

Diego Alonso, born on 16 April 1975, took over as Uruguay's national coach from Óscar Washington Tabárez in the closing stages of the FIFA World Cup qualifying campaign. Alonso, as a player, had played in attack seven times between 1999 and 2001 and with clubs in Uruguay, Argentina, Spain, Mexico and China, before retiring in 2011. He returned home to launch his coaching career with his original club, Bella Vista, and went on to work in Paraguay, Mexico and the USA. Most notably, Alonso guided both Mexican clubs Pachuca and Monterrey to success in the Concacaf Champions League.

The Uruguayans had dominated international football in the first half of the 20th century. Early successes in the South American Championship were followed by victory in the 1924 Olympics in Amsterdam. Uruguay repeated the success in 1928 in Paris and two years later as the host nation swept to victory in the first World Cup.

The side of the 1920s and 1930s contained many of Uruguay's all-time greats: skipper José Nasazzi, half-backs José Andrade, Lorenzo Fernández and Álvaro Gestido, and outstanding forwards Héctor Castro, Pedro Cea and Héctor Scarone.

In 1950, Uruguay reclaimed their status as champions by defeating hosts Brazil 2-1 in the final in Rio de Janeiro's Maracanã. Now, their inspirations were inside forward Juan Schiaffino, wing-half Víctor Andrade, captain and centre-half Obdulio Varela, plus match-winner Alcides Ghiggia at outside right.

They were fourth in 1954 and 1970, though subsequent World Cups proved largely disappointing despite the efforts of star forwards such as Fernando Morena and Enzo Francescoli. Finally, in 2010, the inspiration of Luis Suárez and Diego Forlán lifted Uruguay back into the last four for the first time in 40 years. They followed up by winning the CONMEBOL *Copa América*, in 2011, for a record 15th time.

In the past, Uruguay's squad was built around the players of Montevideo's two great clubs, Peñarol and Nacional, who have dominated the domestic game and collected a host of international trophies. Now, coach Diego Alonso draws his squad from a wide range of clubs in Argentina, Brazil, Colombia, England, Italy, Portugal, Spain, Turkey and the USA.

They have vast experience, with several players boasting a century or

ABOVE: Uruguay were FIFA World Cup champions in 1930 and 1950.

⬢ ONES TO WATCH

EDINSON CAVANI
BORN: 14 FEBRUARY 1987
CLUB: MANCHESTER UNITED
(ENG)

Edinson Cavani is a lethal striker. He was a Uruguayan champion with Danubio, before landing the *Coppa Italia* with Napoli. He won 21 French domestic trophies during a seven-year spell with Paris Saint-Germain, before moving to Manchester United in 2020. Cavani scored 14 goals in 20 age-group appearances for Uruguay, before making his senior debut against Colombia in 2008. He led Uruguay's attack at the 2010, 2014 and 2018 World Cup finals and was a winner with the *Celeste* in the CONMEBOL *Copa América* in 2011.

DIEGO GODÍN
BORN: 16 FEBRUARY 1986
CLUB: ATLÉTICO MINEIRO
(BRA)

Diego Godín, Uruguay's veteran captain and defensive anchor, has made more than 150 appearances for his country. He has played at three FIFA World Cups and was a CONMEBOL *Copa América* champion in 2011. His club career brought eight national and international trophies with Atlético Madrid, for whom he made more than 300 appearances. He began back home with Cerro and Nacional, then starred in Spain with both Villarreal and Atlético Madrid, before moving on to Inter and Cagliari, and then to Brazil with Atlético Mineiro.

RECORD AT PREVIOUS TOURNAMENTS

1930	CHAMPIONS
1934	DID NOT ENTER
1938	DID NOT ENTER
1950	CHAMPIONS
1954	FOURTH PLACE
1958	DID NOT QUALIFY
1962	FIRST ROUND
1966	QUARTER-FINALS
1970	FOURTH PLACE
1974	FIRST ROUND
1978	DID NOT QUALIFY
1982	DID NOT QUALIFY
1986	ROUND OF 16
1990	ROUND OF 16
1994	DID NOT QUALIFY
1998	DID NOT QUALIFY
2002	FIRST ROUND
2006	DID NOT QUALIFY
2010	FOURTH PLACE
2014	ROUND OF 16
2018	QUARTER-FINALS

more of international caps, including goalkeeper Fernando Muslera, defenders such as captain Diego Godín and Martín Cáceres, as well as forwards Suárez and Edinson Cavani.

South America's qualifying tournament comprised a mini-league featuring all ten members of the CONMEBOL regional confederation. The busy schedule was complicated by the COVID-19 pandemic, which saw many of the initial matches postponed and led to the international windows featuring three games instead of two.

Suárez, with a penalty, and Maxi Gómez, in stoppage time, struck the goals that earned Uruguay an opening 2-1 victory over Chile in Montevideo's historic Estadio Centenario in October 2020. A successive defeat in Ecuador was followed by victory in Colombia, then defeat at home to Brazil. Further setbacks were points dropped in three successive draws against Paraguay, Venezuela and Bolivia. A later sequence of four successive defeats, concluding with a 3-0 beating by ten-man Bolivia, left Uruguay three places below the automatic qualifying positions.

Subsequently, Alonso's appointment as national coach brought the desired change of fortune. Victories over Paraguay, Venezuela and Peru secured an all-important qualifying slot with one match still to play. Midfielder Giorgian de Arrascaeta from Brazil's Flamengo scored the lone goal against Peru, which lifted Uruguay over the line.

Suárez, with eight goals, was Uruguay's leading marksman in qualifying as the Atlético Madrid striker had been in the 2014 campaign. His country's dependence on his leadership and goals was illustrated by the fact that De Arrascaeta, with five goals, was their second-top marksman. Next came Cavani and Federico Valverde, with two apiece.

KOREA REPUBLIC

Korea Republic made history in 2002, when they reached the semi-finals of the FIFA World Cup as co-hosts. Matching that achievement provides the inspiration for the *Taeguk Warriors*, who are set to appear in the competition for the tenth successive time.

COACH
PAULO BENTO

Paulo Bento, born on 20 June 1969, is an experienced Portuguese tactician who took up the Korea Republic coaching role in August 2018, succeeding Shin Tae-yong. Bento was a midfielder whose club career featured spells with both Lisbon rivals, Benfica and Sporting. His 35 national-team appearances included games at UEFA EURO 2000 and the 2002 FIFA World Cup™. Bento's senior coaching career began with Sporting, before he led Portugal to the semi-finals of UEFA EURO 2012 and to the 2014 FIFA World Cup. He later coached Brazil's Cruzeiro, Greece's Olympiacos and China PR's Chongqing Lifan.

The Koreans from the south of the peninsula first made their mark on the international stage by reaching the World Cup in Switzerland in 1954, six years after the country was formed. Continuing to play a leading role in the development of international football in the east, they won the first two AFC Asian Cups in 1956 and 1960.

The domestic game then marked time for two decades, until the creation of a professional league was rewarded with regular appearances at successive World Cups from 1986 onwards. Key players in the 1980s and 1990s included powerful central defender Hong Myung-bo and Germany-based forward Cha Bum-kun, whose son, Cha Du-ri, would emulate him as a World Cup footballer.

A further decisive step forward came in 1996, when the country was awarded co-hosting rights for the 2002 FIFA World Cup along with Japan. Dutch coach Guus Hiddink was appointed as national manager at the start of 2001 and achieved remarkable success in a relatively short space of time. Roared on by their passionate supporters, Korea Republic defeated Poland 2-0, played out a 1-1 draw with the USA and then pipped Portugal 1-0 to progress beyond the group stage.

Victories over Italy and Spain (the latter courtesy of a penalty shoot-out) earned them a place in history as the only Asian nation to reach the FIFA World Cup semi-finals. The *Taeguk Warriors* finished a proud fourth.

Building on that achievement has proved challenging. The furthest Korea Republic have progressed since 2002 has been the round of 16 in South Africa in 2010, when they were edged 2-1 by Uruguay. Their dreams were ended in the group stage in both 2014

ABOVE: Korea Republic made their finals debut in 1954.

⬢ ONES TO WATCH

KIM YOUNG-GWON
BORN: 27 FEBRUARY 1990
CLUB: ULSAN HYUNDAI

Kim has played around 90 times in central defence for Korea Republic since his debut in 2010. He rose to prominence with Tokyo and Omiya Ardija in Japan. At China PR's Guangzhou Evergrande he won two AFC Champions League trophies and six Chinese top-flight titles. A move back to Japan with Gamba Osaka was followed by his return home with Ulsan. Kim helped his country win bronze at the 2012 Olympic Games and finish runners-up at the 2015 AFC Asian Cup. At the 2018 FIFA World Cup, Kim opened the scoring in the win over Germany.

LEE JAE-SUNG
BORN: 10 AUGUST 1992
CLUB: MAINZ (GER)

Lee Jae-sung was named the player of the tournament for his performances on the wing and in attacking midfield when Korea Republic won the 2017 EAFF E-1 Football Championship. He had already been a senior international for two years and won the AFC Champions League in 2016, as well as three K League titles with Jeonbuk Hyundai. He then transferred to Germany with Holstein Kiel, whom he led to the German Cup semi-finals, before joining Mainz. Lee played the full 90 minutes in all of his team's matches at the 2018 FIFA World Cup in Russia.

RECORD AT PREVIOUS TOURNAMENTS

1930	DID NOT EXIST
1934	DID NOT EXIST
1938	DID NOT EXIST
1950	DID NOT ENTER
1954	FIRST ROUND
1958	REFUSED ENTRY
1962	DID NOT QUALIFY
1966	DID NOT ENTER
1970	DID NOT QUALIFY
1974	DID NOT QUALIFY
1978	DID NOT QUALIFY
1982	DID NOT QUALIFY
1986	FIRST ROUND
1990	FIRST ROUND
1994	FIRST ROUND
1998	FIRST ROUND
2002	FOURTH PLACE
2006	FIRST ROUND
2010	SECOND ROUND
2014	FIRST ROUND
2018	FIRST ROUND

and 2018. Four years ago, in Russia, they narrowly missed out on qualifying for the round of 16, despite a dramatic 2-0 victory over defending champions Germany in their last game.

In other competitions, the country can point to five successes in the Asian Games – most recently in 2018 – and another five in the East Asian Football Federation (EAFF) E-1 Football Championship, as well as a bronze medal at the 2012 Olympic Games.

The Asian qualifying competition for the FIFA World Cup Qatar 2022 was severely disrupted by the effects of the COVID-19 pandemic, which forced repeated match postponements and tournament adjustments. Korea Republic's third-placed status among Asia's member associations within the FIFA/Coca-Cola Men's World Ranking meant they were granted a bye into the second round. Here, they were drawn against Korea DPR, Lebanon, Sri Lanka and Turkmenistan.

Korea DPR withdrew over COVID-19 health security concerns and Korea Republic seized top place in the group decisively. They won five of their six matches and drew the other, scoring 22 goals and conceding only one. This took them into the third round, namely Group A, from which the top two teams would qualify directly.

Coach Paulo Bento's team were held to a goalless draw by Iraq in front of their own fans in Seoul in the opening match, but made amends with narrow victories over Lebanon (again) and Syria. A second-half goal from Son Heung-min earned them a 1-1 draw in IR Iran, before a winning sequence against the United Arab Emirates, Iraq, Lebanon and Syria. The 2-0 victory over Syria in Dubai sealed their place at the World Cup, with Kim Jin-su and Kwon Chang-hoon scoring the all-important goals.

FIFA WORLD CUP
Qatar2022™

FIFA WORLD CUP SUPERSTARS

The FIFA World Cup opens up the greatest football stage for the greatest of players. Kylian Mbappé of France and veteran superstars such as Portugal's Cristiano Ronaldo and Argentina's Lionel Messi will lead the parade in Qatar. Mbappé's explosion four years ago illustrates how each new World Cup inspires new heroes who claim global attention and admiration.

ALPHONSO DAVIES

Alphonso Davies shot to international attention with his outstanding performances as an attacking left wing-back when his German club, Bayern Munich, won the UEFA Champions League in 2020.

FACTS AND FIGURES

Born:..................2 November 2000
Position: .... Wing–back
Clubs:. Vancouver Whitecaps (CAN), Bayern Munich (GER)
Caps (goals): 30 (10)

His swashbuckling style of play provided an early warning of a new generation of Canadian players who would go on to take their national team to the FIFA World Cup finals for the first time since 1986.

Davies was born in a refugee camp in Ghana and moved with his Liberian family to Canada, and Edmonton, when he was five years old. At 14, he joined the Whitecaps Academy, obtained Canadian citizenship and became the then youngest player to sign a professional MLS contract a year later. In 2016, Davies became the first player born in this century to play Major League Soccer.

In 2018, Davies was named Vancouver Whitecaps' player of the year and, after his reputation spread far beyond North America, he was transferred to Bayern at the start of the following year for USD 24m. This was then a record for an MLS player. Davies proved an almost instant success in German football. Within 18 months, he had won a young-player-of-the-year prize after helping Bayern to a magnificent treble of the UEFA Champions League, German *Bundesliga* and German cup.

Davies, as a teenager, was selected for a number of age-group squads by Canada. On the same day he obtained Canadian citizenship, he was selected for a senior friendly against Curaçao. He duly became, at 16, Canada's youngest-ever international. He then became the youngest marksman in Concacaf Gold Cup history when he scored twice for Canada in a 4-2 defeat of French Guyana.

The goals and the milestones kept on coming. In October 2019, Davies helped Canada defeat the USA for the first time in 34 years in the Concacaf Nations League. He scored the first goal in a 2-0 victory. Later, he featured in the Canadian squad who finished top of their final Concacaf qualifying group to reach the World Cup in Qatar. He celebrates his 22nd birthday shortly before the start of the finals, having already played more than 30 times for his country and reached double figures in goals.

> **"In addition to his speed on the pitch, he's very adept defensively, he sets up goals in attack and scores some himself. He's on a very good path."**
>
> HANSI FLICK, Germany coach

VIRGIL VAN DIJK

Virgil van Dijk has proved an inspirational leader as well as goalscorer from the role of central defender with both the Netherlands and in his club career. He was The Best FIFA Men's Player runner-up in 2019.

Van Dijk's height renders him a commanding figure under pressure. His cool head and vision of the game allow him to organise fellow defenders under pressure and his pace provides the bonus of speed to support midfield and attack when his team are in possession.

These qualities have earned Van Dijk league and league cup-winning medals in Scotland with Celtic then further success in England with Liverpool. Van Dijk was a dominant figure in the *Reds'* 2019 treble of UEFA Champions League, Super Cup and FIFA Club World Cup. One year later and Van Dijk helped power Liverpool to their first domestic league crown in 30 years.

After rising through the U-19s and U-21s, Van Dijk made his senior Netherlands debut against Kazakhstan in October 2015 in the UEFA EURO qualifying competition. He was appointed national team captain by the Netherlands' then-coach Ronald Koeman in March 2018.

The Netherlands were absent from the finals of both the UEFA EURO in 2016 and the FIFA World Cup in 2018, so Van Dijk's national team ambitions were put on hold. In 2019, he led the Netherlands to the final of the inaugural UEFA Nations League, where they finished runners-up to hosts Portugal. Unluckily, he missed the finals of the delayed UEFA EURO 2020 last year because of injury.

Van Dijk, born in Breda, played at youth level with Willem II of Tilburg and then Groningen. His early career was interrupted by serious illness, but he recovered to fulfil his early promise and was sold in 2013 to Scottish champions Celtic. Two years later, Van Dijk flew south to the English Premier League to join Southampton. A transfer to Liverpool in January 2018 for GBP 75m was then a world record for a defender.

In 2019, Van Dijk was voted player of the year by other Premier League players and then as UEFA Men's Player of the Year ahead of Lionel Messi and Cristiano Ronaldo. Liverpool manager Jürgen Klopp described Van Dijk at the time as "the world's best defender".

FACTS AND FIGURES

Born: ....8 July 1991
Position: .... Central defender
Clubs: .... Groningen (NET), Celtic (SCO), Southampton (ENG), Liverpool (ENG)
Caps (goals): 44 (5)

"I played with some of the greatest defenders but I feel unlucky not to have played alongside van Dijk. Virgil will soon be the best defender in the history of football."

PAOLO MALDINI, former Italy and AC Milan defender

KEVIN DE BRUYNE

Kevin de Bruyne's skill, vision, work ethic and goals have been key factors in Belgium's long-running command of the FIFA/Coca-Cola World Ranking and the threat posed by the *Red Devils* at every major tournament.

FACTS AND FIGURES

Born:..........................28 June 1991
Position: ....Midfield
Clubs:.....................KRC Genk (BEL),
Chelsea (ENG),
Werder Bremen (GER),
Wolfsburg (GER),
Manchester City (ENG)
Caps (goals): 104 (50)

The career of a future world football superstar began with his hometown KVE Drongen in central Belgium. Quickly, he progressed up the ladder with KAA Gent and KRC Genk with whom he became national champion. Then it was on to Chelsea in the English Premier League before a move to Germany on loan with Werder Bremen and a EUR 30m transfer to Wolfsburg.

De Bruyne's outstanding displays for both club and country earned a return to English football with Manchester City in 2015. The EUR 65m fee was then a record for a Belgian footballer. The subsequent seven seasons under first Manuel Pellegrini but then, significantly, Pep Guardiola, have seen De Bruyne's career striding from strength to strength.

He and City together have nine domestic trophies and have won three Premier League titles, five League Cups and an FA Cup with the club. Individual honours have included awards as footballer of the year in Germany, sportsman of the year in Belgium, premier league player of the season and UEFA Champions League midfielder of the season. Manchester City manager Guardiola has described De Bruyne as "one of the best players I've ever seen in my life".

De Bruyne played for Belgium at U-18, U-19 and U-21 levels, before making his senior debut in August 2010 away to Finland. His first goal for his country followed two months later away to Serbia. Subsequently, De Bruyne established himself in the starting line-up ahead of the 2014 FIFA World Cup finals. In Brazil, De Bruyne served up a goal and an assist in a round-of-16 victory over the USA before Belgium's quarter-final exit.

De Bruyne and Belgium were halted at the quarter-finals again at UEFA EURO 2016, before they went one round better and finished third at the 2018 FIFA World Cup in Russia. He provided an assist for two-goal Romelu Lukaku in Belgium's opening 3-0 win over Panama, scored the second goal in their 2-1 quarter-final victory over Brazil and was named the man of the match.

> **"We've had six years together here with Kevin. He has something unique in the world. We all know it. Kevin is an exceptional player."**
>
> PEP GUARDIOLA, Manchester City manager

HARRY KANE

Harry Kane top-scored with six goals at the 2018 FIFA World Cup to earn the right to rank alongside star England marksmen of the past such as Geoff Hurst, Gary Lineker and Alan Shearer.

FACTS AND FIGURES

Born:........................ 28 July 1993
Position: .... Striker
Clubs:..... Tottenham Hotspur (ENG)
Caps (goals): 67 (48)

Kane joined Tottenham as a boy after being released by Arsenal. He turned professional in 2010 and had loan spells with four other clubs before returning to make his mark with Spurs in the 2013-2014 season. Since then, he has scored more than 200 goals for the *Lilywhites* and has been the Premier League's top scorer on three occasions. Kane also struck five goals to help Tottenham to the UEFA Champions League final in 2018-2019.

This goalscoring consistency is matched by Kane's leadership in the demanding role of centre-forward for both club and country. He steadily worked his way up the national-team ladder, representing England at U-17, U-19, U-20 and U-21 levels.

Kane played and scored at the FIFA U-20 World Cup in 2013 and was a regular with the U-21s when he made his senior debut against Lithuania in a UEFA EURO 2016 qualifying match. Kane needed only 80 seconds to open his goalscoring account. His first start for the senior team followed days later in a 1-1 draw with Italy in Turin.

From this point on, Kane has been a first-choice starter for England. After being handed the captain's armband, he led by example at the 2018 FIFA World Cup, where his six goals fired the *Three Lions* to the semi-finals. Kane followed up by scoring in each of England's qualifying matches en route to UEFA EURO 2020. He added a further four goals at the tournament, where England finished runners-up.

More milestones were to come in the qualifying competition for Qatar 2022. Kane scored four goals in the 10-0 victory over San Marino with which the *Three Lions* secured qualification, in the process of becoming one of only four players to have bagged a hat-trick in back-to-back matches for England and the first since the 1950s. His overall total of 12 goals established him as the joint-leading scorer in the European qualifiers, with the Netherlands' Memphis Depay. That unerring eye for goal will prove crucial for England.

> **"Harry's finishing quality is top – as good as anyone I've played with or worked with. We're fortunate to have him."**
>
> GARETH SOUTHGATE, England manager

ROBERT LEWANDOWSKI

Robert Lewandowski's insatiable hunger for goals has been rewarded by a double award as The Best FIFA Men's Player of 2020 and 2021 plus a never-ending stream of decisive strikes for club and country.

Poland's captain and centre-forward has scored a record 70-plus goals since registering the first on his debut as a 20-year-old against San Marino. Left far behind in his magnificent wake have been the achievements of 1970s stars Włodek Lubański (48 goals), Grzegorz Lato (45) and Kazimierz Deyna (41).

As Polish Football Association President Zbigniew Boniek said: "Robert is a great and fantastic football player. It is impossible to compare him with anyone. He is like a postage stamp, his value will grow the longer time goes on."

Lewandowski, remarkably quick and nimble for a man of his height, first made the Polish game sit up and take notice when, as an 18-year-old, he was leading marksman in both third and second divisions with Znicz Pruszków. A 2008 transfer to Lech Poznań saw him win the league, cup and super cup and another top-scorer prize, which secured a move to Germany with Borussia Dortmund in 2010.

Goals and glory followed to the tune of two German *Bundesliga* titles, one cup and a runners-up medal in the UEFA Champions League. A further move to Bayern Munich in 2014 brought a further seven successive league titles, eight cups and league cups plus an international treble in 2020 of UEFA Champions League, UEFA Super Cup and FIFA Club World Cup.

Lewandowski, a UNICEF Goodwill Ambassador, has been *Bundesliga* top scorer six times, player of the season twice and Polish footballer of the year nine times. He has scored more than 300 *Bundesliga* goals, second only in the all-time rankings to Bayern icon Gerd Müller.

Simultaneously, Lewandowski's goals kept flowing for Poland. He led Poland's attack as co-hosts, with Ukraine, for the 2012 UEFA European Championship and scored the tournament's opening goal against Greece. A year later, he was appointed the national captain.

Lewandowski was as lethal as ever in the qualifiers for UEFA EURO 2016, when he scored 13 goals to equal the tournament record. He followed up with a remarkable 16 in European qualifying for the 2018 World Cup and another nine en route to Qatar.

FACTS AND FIGURES

Born: .... 21 August 1988
Position: .... Centre–forward
Clubs: .... Znicz Pruszków (POL),
Lech Poznań (POL),
Borussia Dortmund (GER),
Bayern Munich (GER)
Caps (goals): 128 (74)

> **"He has the qualities which compare with the biggest stars. He has the nose of a goalscorer and his achievements are in a class of their own."**
>
> ZBIGNIEW BONIEK, ex-PZPN President

SADIO MANÉ

Sadio Mané's commitment to Senegal's footballing cause was rewarded in dramatic fashion twice inside two months in early 2022.

In February, the *Lions of Teranga* defeated Egypt on penalties to win the Africa Cup of Nations and then, at the end of the following month, Mané converted the last decisive spot kick in another shoot-out victory over Egypt – this time taking himself back, with Senegal, to a second successive FIFA World Cup finals.

Mané was born in the village of Bambali from where his love of football and teenage talent took him 400km to the capital, Dakar. Here he joined the Generation Foot youth academy whose partnership with French club Metz saw him move to Europe in 2011. Less than a year later, Mané made his Metz debut, in the second division.

Metz were relegated in 2012 but Mané's career was heading upwards. He was sold to Red Bull Salzburg for a Metz club record of EUR 4m and within three months had started repaying the investment with hat-tricks in both the Austrian league and cup. Mané's goals fired Salzburg to a league and cup double in 2014 and earned him a further career-enhancing transfer to Southampton in England.

His club career continued from strength to strength. He scored 21 goals in two seasons with Southampton, including a remarkable three goals in two minutes 56 seconds in a 6–1 win over Aston Villa. This was the fastest hat-trick in Premier League history and prompted a transfer race which was won by Liverpool in the summer of 2016. The fee was GBP 34m, then the highest price for an African player.

Liverpool, under the management of Jürgen Klopp, proved a perfect fit for Mané in forging an irresistible attacking unit with Roberto Firmino and Mohamed Salah. In 2019, they won the UEFA Champions League and Mané was subsequently voted African Footballer of the Year. A year further on and he became only the third African to reach 100 Premier League goals.

He started all three matches at the 2018 FIFA World Cup finals and scored Senegal's opening goal in a 2-2 draw with Japan. He returns to the finals as an African champion and with around 30 goals to his credit after his 10-year international career.

> "Sadio is a top, top player. He reads the game, he has an eye for an opening and he is so quick to make it count. He is so difficult to defend against."
>
> JÜRGEN KLOPP, Liverpool manager

FACTS AND FIGURES

Born: ....10 April 1992
Position: .... Forward
Clubs: ....Metz (FRA),
RB Salzburg (AUS),
Southampton (ENG),
Liverpool (ENG)
Caps (goals): 87 (29)

KYLIAN MBAPPÉ

Kylian Mbappé is one of the most exciting young stars to have exploded on international football for many years. He was acclaimed as the best young player after France's victory at the 2018 FIFA World Cup.

Mbappé was born in Paris and took his first steps in football in the suburban Paris club AS Bondy, where his father, Wilfried, was a coach. His talent brought a move to the Clairefontaine national academy and attracted scouts and offers from leading clubs in England, Germany and Spain. Eventually, he accepted an offer from Monaco, where he became their youngest debutant at 16 years 347 days.

Goals and even hat-tricks followed as Mbappé's star shone ever more brightly in French domestic competitions as well as in the UEFA Champions League. Mbappé's goals led Monaco to the French league title and Champions League semi-finals in 2017 after which he joined PSG, initially on loan, and subsequently for EUR 150m. Thus, he became the second-most expensive player of all time.

Mbappé lived up to expectations by helping PSG win the French league title in each of his first three seasons as well as the treble of league, French cup and league cup in two of them. His mixture of power, pace and goals earned him national player of the year awards in 2018 and 2019.

France and Mbappé won the UEFA U-19 crown in 2016 and he made his debut at senior national-team level the following year, still only 18. At the 2018 FIFA World Cup finals, Mbappé became the youngest French player to score at a World Cup and the second teenager, after Pelé 60 years earlier, to score in a World Cup final. He finished as the joint second-highest goalscorer as France won the tournament, and received the Best Young Player and French Player of the Year awards for his performances.

He went from strength to strength in 2020 despite the upheavals enforced by the COVID-19 pandemic. He was leading marksman with 18 goals, as PSG were crowned champions after the French season's premature conclusion. Mbappé finished level with Monaco's Wissam Ben Yedder, but was assigned the prize through a superior-goals-per-game ratio. In 2021, Mbappé scored the winning goal, as France defeated Spain 2-1 to win the final of the UEFA Nations League.

FACTS AND FIGURES

Born:............... 20 December 1998
Position: .... Forward
Clubs:..................... Monaco (FRA),
Paris Saint–Germain (FRA)
Caps (goals): 53 (24)

"There's not many people who will make me jump out of my seat or make me scream, but Mbappé is one of those. It's all about natural instinct."

THIERRY HENRY, France record goalscorer

LIONEL MESSI

Lionel Messi may be approaching his last FIFA World Cup but his record-breaking brilliance has shown little sign of waning during the latest stage of a career which has attracted a flood of superlatives.

FACTS AND FIGURES

Born:..........................24 June 1987
Position: .... Forward
Clubs:.................. Barcelona (SPA),
Paris Saint–Germain (FRA)
Caps (goals): 158 (80)

Argentina boasts many of the greatest footballers in the game's history, from early FIFA World Cup heroes such as Luisito Monti and Raimundo Orsi to Alfredo Di Stefano and Ángel Labruna, then on to World Cup-winners such as Mario Kempes in 1978 and the incomparable Diego Maradona in 1986.

Messi's own place in the pantheon of the game owes everything not merely to his skill on the ball allied to selfless teamwork but to the sheer weight of statistics which cement his reputation.

The *Atomic Flea* left Newell's Old Boys in Rosario at 13 to spend 18 years with Barcelona before transferring his talents to Paris Saint-Germain. Messi moved to French football in August 2021, weeks after leading Argentina to success in the CONMEBOL *Copa América* for the first time. His individual dominance of the tournament was such that he was hailed as both best player and joint four-goal top scorer. A 1-0 win over hosts Brazil in the Maracanã stadium went some way to making amends for runners-up disappointments in 2007, 2015 and 2016.

Messi has won the FIFA top-player prize on six occasions to burnish a club record, which includes more than 34 club titles at international and Spanish domestic levels, plus well over 100 individual prizes and top-scorer awards, as well as the European Golden Shoe as Europe's leading league marksman on six occasions. The individual prizes included the Golden Ball for finest individual at the World Cup finals in 2014 when Argentina finished runners-up.

He has scored more than 700 goals in his career, with records for most goals in *La Liga* (474), most goals in one Spanish league season (50) and an overall European mainstream season (73), as well as most hat-tricks in *La Liga* (36). He is also the record non-European marksman in the history of the UEFA Champions League.

On the worldwide stage, Messi reigns supreme as Argentina's record international and all-time leading goalscorer. He inspired Argentina's victory in the FIFA U-20 World Cup in 2005 in the Netherlands and was an Olympic Games gold medallist in 2008 in Beijing. Only the World Cup remains to complete his record-breaking sweep.

"Messi will always be Messi. He will never be down or lack morale. He is always very competitive and even more so with Argentina."

MARIO KEMPES, 1978 FIFA World Cup™ winner

TAKUMI MINAMINO

Takumi Minamino, still only 27, can look back on a wealth of international experience that has seen him develop into one of the most exciting footballers in the Asian game.

FACTS AND FIGURES

Born:.................16 January 1995
Position: .... Midfield
Clubs:...............Cerezo Osaka (JPN),
RB Salzburg (AUS),
Southampton (ENG),
Liverpool (ENG)
Caps (goals): 37 (17)

His potential was never questioned by his coaches with both club and country after he starred initially with Japan's U-15 and U-16 teams.

Minamino's reputation rests on his skill and pace on the left flank, from full-back or as an attacking midfielder, and he can score goals as well as create them. On his debut in the AFC U-16 Championship, he scored three goals in the group stage and then another in a quarter-final victory over Iraq, before Japan eventually fell in the semi-finals. He was the event's joint top scorer.

Further goals followed in the FIFA U-17 World Cup in 2011 and AFC Asian U-19 finals in 2014. By then, Minamino had already established himself in the J.League with Cerezo Osaka, who transferred him to European football with RB Salzburg in January 2016. Where Japan's senior national-team squad is concerned, Minamino was called up in a preliminary selection ahead of the 2014 FIFA World Cup finals, before finally making his debut as a substitute in a friendly against IR Iran in October 2015.

Minamino was one of the stars of the 2019 AFC Asian Cup. He played a decisive role in the semi-finals with two assists in a victory over IR Iran, but was on the losing side, despite scoring in the final against Qatar.

By now, his European club career had progressed. He helped RB Salzburg win ten trophies in the Austrian league and cup and reach the semi-finals of the UEFA Europa League before transferring to Liverpool in January 2020. Minamino went out on loan to Southampton before returning to Anfield and becoming a League Cup winner in 2022.

Minamino found competition for starting places intense at Liverpool, but was able to prove his quality when Sadio Mané and Mohamed Salah were absent on national-team duties at the Africa Cup of Nations. Japanese fans were already aware of his ability after more than 80 appearances at all international levels across the age groups since he was only 15 in 2010.

> "He is very disciplined and wants to do everything exactly as it is explained to him. He has had the right football education and he never hides."
>
> PETER ZEIDLER, ex-RB Salzburg coach

LUKA MODRIĆ

Luka Modrić, Croatia's long-serving captain and playmaker, won the FIFA Golden Ball as the best player at the 2018 FIFA World Cup after his skill and inspiration led his team-mates to the final in Moscow.

Finishing as runners-up to France was the closest Croatia had come to seizing one of the major international prizes. But, with Modrić commanding and cajoling in midfield, they have always been among the most threatening challengers and that will be the case again in Qatar.

Modrić was playing for Dinamo Zagreb when he was called up first for the national team against Argentina in March 2006. Three months later, he made two appearances as a substitute in the group-stage exchanges at the FIFA World Cup in Germany. Modrić was then at the heart of the action when Croatia reached the quarter-finals at the finals of the UEFA EURO in 2008.

Croatia failed to progress beyond the group stage in 2012 and also at the FIFA World Cup in 2014. In 2016, however, they reached the round of 16 at the UEFA EURO in France, where Modrić became the first Croat to have scored a goal in two European finals tournaments. He was then captain for the memorable 2018 FIFA World Cup campaign.

Modrić has enjoyed a trophy-laden career at club level. Initially, he was three times a national league champion and twice a domestic cup winner with Dinamo Zagreb. In 2008, he transferred to Tottenham Hotspur and was voted the club's player of the year in 2011. A year later, he was sold to Real Madrid for EUR 30m. Only two days later, he won his first trophy in Spain, as Madrid beat Barcelona in the Spanish Super Cup.

All together, Modrić has celebrated silverware on 17 occasions. These triumphs have included three victories in the FIFA Club World Cup and four in the UEFA Champions League. Modrić has been hailed twice as UEFA's best midfielder of the season and he also became the first Croatia player included in the annual FIFA FIFPRO World XI squads. In 2018, he won the Best FIFA Men's Player and Ballon d'Or awards, the first star in more than a decade to break the duopoly of Lionel Messi and Cristiano Ronaldo.

FACTS AND FIGURES

Born:.................9 September 1985
Position: .... Midfield
Clubs:...........Dinamo Zagreb (CRO),
Zrinjski Mostar (BIH),
Inter Zaprešić (CRO),
Tottenham Hotspur (ENG),
Real Madrid (SPA)
Caps (goals): 146 (20)

"Luka Modrić is a legend. He has always taken great care of himself and his fitness levels, so in his career, he has not had any major injuries. That can tell you a lot."

CARLO ANCELOTTI, Real Madrid manager

MANUEL NEUER

Manuel Neuer has inspired a tactical revolution with his sweeper-keeper style of play, which often makes it appear that Germany's national team and his club Bayern Munich have an extra player out on the pitch.

FACTS AND FIGURES

Born:......................27 March 1986
Position:....................Goalkeeper
Clubs:.......................Schalke (GER)
Bayern Munich (GER)
Caps (goals):......................108 (0)

A FIFA World Cup-winner in 2014, Neuer has been a fixture in Germany's goal since they reached the semi-finals in South Africa four years earlier. He celebrated his 100th senior international against Latvia in June 2021. By that time, he had long overhauled the previous goalkeeping record of 95 caps, set by Bayern hero Sepp Maier. Neuer has also recorded more than 40 clean sheets for his country.

Neuer, twice voted domestic footballer of the year, progressed via Germany's U-19s and then the U-21s, with whom he won the UEFA European Championship in 2009. Already Neuer had been called into the senior national team by coach Joachim Low, making his debut on an Asian tour against the United Arab Emirates.

The FIFA World Cup 2022 will be Neuer's fourth outing at the pinnacle of the game. He was first-choice when *Die Mannschaft* reached the semi-finals in 2010, won the Golden Glove award as best goalkeeper in the victorious 2014 campaign and was there again as captain in Russia four years later.

Neuer made his name and developed his modern game style with his local club Schalke from Gelsenkirchen. He helped Schalke win the German cup once, before securing five more victories in the competition after transferring to Bayern Munich in 2011. Those safe hands have now scooped up around 30 trophies at national and international level.

Neuer's most outstanding campaign at club level was in 2019-2020, when Bayern landed the domestic treble of *Bundesliga*, DFB Cup and league cup, plus the UEFA Champions League, UEFA Super Cup and finally the FIFA Club World Cup. Not surprisingly, he was also voted FIFA Men's Goalkeeper that year, too.

Bayern beat French club Paris Saint-Germain in the Champions League final. After the game, PSG's German coach Thomas Tuchel described Neuer as "having taken goalkeeping to a new level". This was echoed by Italian hero Gianluigi Buffon who said: "Neuer is one of the greatest of modern goalkeepers."

"We always had great goalkeepers but if you look at everything he's won then you can also say he is one of the best there has ever been on our planet."

OLIVER KAHN, ex-Germany goalkeeper

NEYMAR

Neymar, the world's most expensive footballer, shoulders once again the hopes and dreams of Brazil as the *Seleção* pursue what would be a record-extending sixth triumph at the FIFA World Cup finals.

His talents were evident from his early teenage years when he was a target for Europe's leading clubs, before deciding that home was where his heart and greatest support lay as he developed his individual style. Now, Neymar ranks as one of Brazil's most acclaimed internationals in terms of both appearances and goals.

As Brazilian footballing great Pelé has acknowledged: "He is a complete player both for the team and because he scores the goals he does. He does it for Brazil and he does it for his clubs."

Pelé's old club Santos provided the launch pad for Neymar. He made his senior debut as a 17-year-old in early 2009. Two years later, he helped Brazil win the South American youth championship and collected the FIFA Puskás Award for the outstanding individual goal of a year in which he and Santos also won the CONMEBOL *Libertadores*. Santos went on to the FIFA Club World Cup. They lost the final to Barcelona, but the Catalans could barely wait to make Neymar their own after Brazil's victory in the FIFA Confederations Cup in 2013.

Barcelona's "MSN" attack – Leo Messi, Luis Suárez and Neymar – wreaked havoc across Europe, while Neymar led Brazil's attack at the FIFA World Cup, CONMEBOL *Copa América* and Olympic Games.

Injury meant that Neymar missed Brazil's 2014 FIFA World Cup semi-final exit, but two years later he played a captain's role at the Olympics in Rio de Janeiro. Neymar converted the winning penalty as the hosts defeated Germany in a shoot-out in the Maracanã to win Olympic gold for the first time.

Brazil then came up disappointingly short for Neymar at the 2018 FIFA World Cup and 2021 CONMEBOL *Copa América,* but his club career went from strength to strength.

Neymar won six national and international titles with Santos and another eight during his four years with Barcelona in Spain, including the FIFA Club World Cup and UEFA Champions League in 2015. A dozen further trophies have cascaded since Neymar's EUR 222m world record-breaking move to Paris Saint-Germain in 2017. Twice, he has been hailed South American footballer of the year.

FACTS AND FIGURES

Born:.................. 5 February 1992
Position: .... Forward
Clubs:........................Santos (BRA),
Barcelona (SPA),
Paris Saint-Germain (FRA)
Caps (goals): 116 (70)

"He is our brightest star of the last 20 years. We have had no other player with Neymar's ability to make a difference and resolve a game on his own."

CAFU, 2002 FIFA World Cup-winning captain

CRISTIANO RONALDO

Cristiano Ronaldo dos Santos Aveiro ranks as one of the greatest players in football history through his stand-alone achievements at national team, club and individual levels.

FACTS AND FIGURES

Born:...................5 February 1985
Position: ....Striker
Clubs:................ Sporting CP (POR),
Manchester United (ENG),
Real Madrid (SPA),
Juventus (ITA),
Manchester United (ENG)
Caps (goals): 184 (115)

Portugal's captain, Cristiano Ronaldo, has claimed a host of world player awards among a plethora of prizes, which have seen him win the FIFA Club World Cup four times, the UEFA Champions League five times – with Manchester United and Real Madrid – the UEFA EURO in 2016 and the UEFA Nations League in 2019.

The Madeira-born forward now claims more than 800 goals in a lethal 20-year career, bringing him from Sporting Clube of Lisbon to league title-winning pinnacles of the club game in England, Spain and Italy. He has set marksmanship records, including a stream of hat-tricks, in the Champions League and has been crowned domestic league leading marksman in England, Spain and Italy.

Along the way, Ronaldo has also far outstripped the goalscoring achievements of Portugal's 1960s legend Eusébio. His status was officially recognised in 2015, when he was named the best Portuguese player ever by his football association.

Ronaldo was 18 in August 2003, when he made his senior debut against Kazakhstan and now ranks as record-holder in terms of both international appearances and goals. The following year, he and Portugal were UEFA EURO runners-up as hosts before his first World Cup saw them finish fourth in Germany in 2006. In 2010, Portugal lost in the round of 16 to Spain, and Brazil in 2014 was a further disappointment when, with Ronaldo hampered by injury, Portugal fell in the group stage.

His personal qualities and those of his team-mates were underlined in 2016 when Portugal won the UEFA EURO. Ronaldo, having scored three goals, was injured early in the final but his reward, as captain, was to hoist aloft the first major trophy in Portugal's history. Ronaldo led Portugal to further success in the 2019 UEFA Nations League in between round-of-16 exits at the 2018 World Cup and 2020 Euro.

Ronaldo's achievements have earned him FIFA's top men's player prize on seven occasions and Portugal's player of the year four times. The airport in his native Madeira has even been renamed in his honour.

> **"His energy and attitude are examples to any young kid. Whether it's his movement, his touch, or his control, everything about him is first class."**
>
> ALAN SHEARER, former England captain

LUIS SUÁREZ

Uruguay has provided world football with a never-ending stream of outstanding players down all the years since the *Celeste* won the inaugural World Cup in 1930.

Centre-forward Luis Suárez has maintained that great tradition in not only his club career but also for Uruguay, in a 16-year national-team era which has brought him an average goal every two games in more than 130 appearances.

Suárez was born in Salto, far to the north-west of Montevideo. His family moved to the capital and he was a star already in his early teenage years with Nacional, one of Uruguay's two great clubs along with Penarol. At 19, Suárez was a Uruguayan champion before he undertook an ambitious transfer to Groningen in the Netherlands.

A year was all it took him to earn a move to Amsterdam with former world and European champions Ajax. Leadership qualities and a natural goalscoring facility quickly saw Suárez become captain and league top scorer. Not only that, but he shot his way to more than a century of club goals to rank alongside Ajax legends such as Dennis Bergkamp, Johan Cruyff and Marco van Basten.

A cascade of brilliant, cheeky and ruthless goals over four seasons prompted a transfer to Liverpool. He scored a further 82 goals in all competitions and, in 2014, was a member of the Uruguay squad who finished fourth at the FIFA World Cup in Brazil. However, he missed the latter stages of the campaign through suspension and left Liverpool for Barcelona on his return to Europe.

More rewards were on the way as Suárez starred as brightly in Barcelona's attack as Lionel Messi and Neymar. Together the trio achieved a five-trophy sweep in the UEFA Champions League, UEFA Super Cup, Spanish league and cup as well as FIFA Club World Cup. After six years in Barcelona, Suárez left for Atlético Madrid in 2020.

Suárez made his debut in the light blue of the *Celeste* at the FIFA U-20 World Cup 2007 and was promoted to the senior squad that same year. Apart from then appearing at three World Cups, Suárez won the CONMEBOL *Copa América* in 2011 when he was also voted player of the tournament.

> **"With Suárez in the team, you felt that whoever you were playing, he was going to win you the game. It didn't matter who it was against."**
>
> STEVEN GERRARD, ex-Liverpool captain

FACTS AND FIGURES

Born:	24 January 1987
Position:	Striker
Clubs:	Nacional (URU), Groningen (NET), Liverpool (ENG), Barcelona (SPA), Atlético Madrid (SPA)
Caps (goals):	130 (67)

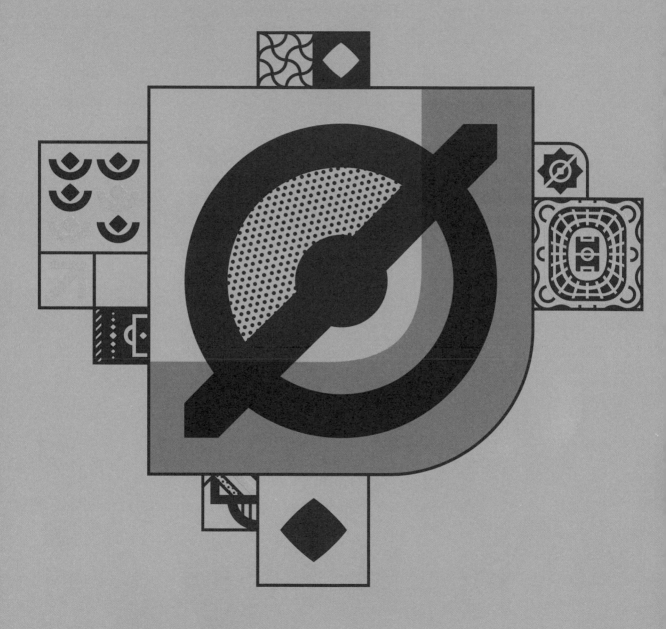

FIFA WORLD CUP
Qatar2022™

FIFA WORLD CUP RECORDS

The FIFA World Cup holds an enduring appeal for fans. Since the inaugural event in Uruguay in 1930, the matches played in both qualifying competitions and the subsequent final tournaments have generated an almost never-ending multiplicity of facts, figures and statistics. Some records have stood for a long time – notably Frenchman Just Fontaine's still unsurpassed feat of scoring 13 goals at the 1958 tournament in Sweden – while others have changed hands from tournament to tournament.

FIFA WORLD CUP TEAM RECORDS

Some countries are regulars on the biggest footballing stage of all – but only eight have experienced the thrill of being crowned the best team in the world.

FIFA WORLD CUP FINALS

YEAR	HOSTS	WINNERS	RUNNERS-UP	SCORE
1930	Uruguay	Uruguay	Argentina	4-2
1934	Italy	Italy	Czechoslovakia	2-1 (a.e.t.)
1938	France	Italy	Hungary	4-2
1950	Brazil	Uruguay	Brazil	2-1
1954	Switzerland	West Germany	Hungary	3-2
1958	Sweden	Brazil	Sweden	5-2
1962	Chile	Brazil	Czechoslovakia	3-1
1966	England	England	West Germany	4-2 (a.e.t.)
1970	Mexico	Brazil	Italy	4-1
1974	West Germany	West Germany	Netherlands	2-1
1978	Argentina	Argentina	Netherlands	3-1 (a.e.t.)
1982	Spain	Italy	West Germany	3-1
1986	Mexico	Argentina	West Germany	3-2
1990	Italy	West Germany	Argentina	1-0
1994	USA	Brazil	Italy	0-0 (a.e.t.; 3-2 on pens)
1998	France	France	Brazil	3-0
2002	Japan/Korea Republic	Brazil	Germany	2-0
2006	Germany	Italy	France	1-1 (a.e.t.; 5-3 on pens)
2010	South Africa	Spain	Netherlands	1-0 (a.e.t.)
2014	Brazil	Germany	Argentina	1-0 (a.e.t.)
2018	Russia	France	Croatia	4-2

ABOVE: Uruguay, first hosts and first winners of the World Cup in 1930.

MOST FIFA WORLD CUP FINAL APPEARANCES

8	Germany
7	Brazil
6	Italy
5	Argentina
3	France
=	Netherlands
2	Czechoslovakia
=	Hungary
=	Uruguay
1	Croatia
=	England
=	Sweden

MOST FIFA WORLD CUP FINAL VICTORIES

5	Brazil
4	Italy
=	Germany
2	Argentina
=	France
=	Uruguay
1	England
=	Spain

MOST FIFA WORLD CUP RUNNERS-UP PLACINGS

4	Germany
3	Argentina
=	Netherlands
2	Brazil
=	Czechoslovakia
=	Hungary
=	Italy
1	Croatia
=	France
=	Sweden

FIFA WORLD CUP ALL-TIME RANKING

FINALS		P	W	D	L	GF	GA	GD	
1	Brazil	21	109	73	18	18	229	105	+124
2	Germany	19	109	67	20	22	226	125	+101
3	Italy	18	83	45	21	17	128	77	+51
4	Argentina	17	81	43	15	23	137	93	+44
5	Mexico	16	57	16	14	27	60	98	−38
6	England	15	69	29	21	19	91	64	+27
7	France	15	66	34	13	19	120	77	+43
8	Spain	15	63	30	15	18	99	72	+27

Based on tournaments, match victories, etc.

ABOVE: West Germany's Jurgen Klinsmann celebrates in 1990.

FIFA WORLD CUP FINAL ATTENDANCES

YEAR	ATTENDANCE	STADIUM
1930	93,000	Estadio Centenario, Montevideo
1934	45,000	Stadio Nazionale del PNF, Rome
1938	60,000	Stade Olympique de Colombes, Paris
1950	173,830–210,000	Estádio do Maracanã, Rio de Janeiro
1954	64,000	Wankdorfstadion, Bern
1958	51,800	Råsunda Fotbollstadion, Solna
1962	68,679	Estadio Nacional, Santiago
1966	98,000	Wembley Stadium, London
1970	107,412	Estadio Azteca, Mexico City
1974	75,200	Olympiastadion, Munich
1978	71,483	Estadio Monumental, Buenos Aires
1982	90,000	Estadio Santiago Bernabéu, Madrid
1986	114,600	Estadio Azteca, Mexico City
1990	73,603	Stadio Olimpico, Rome
1994	94,194	Rose Bowl, Pasadena
1998	75,000	Stade de France, Paris
2002	69,029	International Stadium, Yokohama
2006	69,000	Olympiastadion, Berlin
2010	84,490	Soccer City, Johannesburg
2014	74,738	Estádio do Maracanã, Rio de Janeiro
2018	78,011	Luzhniki Stadium, Moscow

FIFA WORLD CUP OVERALL TOURNAMENT ATTENDANCES

YEAR	TOTAL ATTENDANCE	AVERAGE ATTENDANCE
1930	434,500	(24,139)
1934	395,000	(21,059)
1938	483,000	(26,833)
1950	1,337,000	(47,091)
1954	943,000	(34,212)
1958	868,000	(26,274)
1962	776,000	(28,096)
1966	1,614,677	(51,094)
1970	1,673,975	(50,124)
1974	1,774,022	(46,685)
1978	1,610,215	(40,688)
1982	1,856,277	(40,572)
1986	2,407,431	(46,026)
1990	2,517,348	(48,391)
1994	3,587,538	(68,991)
1998	2,785,100	(43,517)
2002	2,705,197	(42,269)
2006	3,352,605	(52,401)
2010	3,178,856	(49,670)
2014	3,386,810	(52,919)
2018	3,031,768	(47,371)
Total:	40,718,319	(42,305)

RIGHT: South Africa's sun shines on Soccer City in Johannesburg during Netherlands' 2–0 victory over Denmark.

FIFA WORLD CUP PLAYER RECORDS

Appearing at the FIFA World Cup final tournament is a career highlight for most players. Many have been fortunate enough to savour the experience on several occasions. Others have only had the privilege once, but have made their mark.

MOST FIFA WORLD CUP FINAL TOURNAMENTS

NUMBER OF TOURNAMENTS	NAME	TEAM	YEARS
5	Gianluigi Buffon	(Italy)	1998*, 2002, 2006, 2010, 2014
=	Antonio Carbajal	(Mexico)	1950, 1954, 1958, 1962, 1966
=	Rafael Márquez	(Mexico)	2002, 2006, 2010, 2014, 2018
=	Lothar Matthäus	(West Germany /Germany)	1982, 1986, 1990, 1994, 1998

* Unused squad member.

LEFT: Mexico goalkeeper Antonio Carbajal was the first man to play in five World Cups.

BELOW: Northern Ireland's Norman Whiteside was the youngest World Cup finalist.

YOUNGEST PLAYERS TO PLAY IN THE WORLD CUP FINAL

NAME	TEAM	AGE OF APPEARANCE
Pelé	(Brazil)	17 years, 249 days in 1958
Giuseppe Bergomi	(Italy)	18 years, 201 days in 1982
Kylian Mbappé	(France)	19 years, 207 days in 2018

YOUNGEST PLAYERS AT THE WORLD CUP FINAL TOURNAMENT

NAME	TEAM	AGE OF APPEARANCE
Norman Whiteside	(Northern Ireland)	17 years, 41 days in 1982
Samuel Eto'o	(Cameroon)	17 years, 99 days in 1998
Femi Opabunmi	(Nigeria)	17 years, 101 days in 2002

OLDEST PLAYERS TO PLAY IN THE WORLD CUP FINAL

NAME	TEAM	AGE AND YEAR
Dino Zoff	(Italy)	40 years, 133 days in 1982
Gunnar Gren	(Sweden)	37 years, 241 days in 1958
Jan Jongbloed	(Netherlands)	37 years, 212 days in 1978

OLDEST PLAYERS AT THE WORLD CUP FINAL TOURNAMENT

NAME	TEAM	AGE AND YEAR
Essam El Hadary	(Egypt)	45 years, 161 days in 2018
Faryd Mondragón	(Colombia)	43 years, 3 days in 2014
Roger Milla	(Cameroon)	42 years, 39 days in 1994

LONGEST PERIODS WITHOUT CONCEDING A GOAL BY GOALKEEPERS IN THE FIFA WORLD CUP FINAL TOURNAMENT

NAME	TEAM	NUMBER OF MINUTES PLAYED WITHOUT CONCEDING AND YEAR(S)
Walter Zenga	(Italy)	517 minutes, 1990
Peter Shilton	(England)	502 minutes, 1986-90
Sepp Maier	(West Germany)	475 minutes, 1974-78

ABOVE: Egypt's Essam El Hadary commands his defence in 2018.

BEST GOALKEEPERS OF THE TOURNAMENT

YEAR	NAME	TEAM
1930	Enrique Ballestrero	(Uruguay)
1934	Ricardo Zamora	(Spain)
1938	František Plánička	(Czechoslovakia)
1950	Roque Máspoli	(Uruguay)
1954	Gyula Grosics	(Hungary)
1958	Harry Gregg	(Northern Ireland)
1962	Viliam Schrojf	(Czechoslovakia)
1966	Gordon Banks	(England)
1970	Ladislao Mazurkiewicz	(Uruguay)
1974	Sepp Maier	(West Germany)
1978	Ubaldo Fillol	(Argentina)
1982	Dino Zoff	(Italy)
1986	Jean-Marie Pfaff	(Belgium)
1990	Gabelo Conejo / Sergio Goycochea	(Costa Rica) / (Argentina)
1994	Michel Preud'homme	(Belgium)
1998	Fabien Barthez	(France)
2002	Oliver Kahn	(Germany)
2006	Gianluigi Buffon	(Italy)
2010	Iker Casillas	(Spain)
2014	Manuel Neuer	(Germany)
2018	Thibaut Courtois	(Belgium)

DOUBLE WINNERS

Players who played on the winning side in two World Cup finals

NAME	TEAM	YEARS
Cafu	(Brazil)	1994, 2002
Didi	(Brazil)	1958, 1962
Giovanni Ferrari	(Italy)	1934, 1938
Garrincha	(Brazil)	1958, 1962
Gilmar	(Brazil)	1958, 1962
Giuseppe Meazza	(Italy)	1934, 1938
Pelé	(Brazil)	1958, 1970
Djalma Santos	(Brazil)	1958, 1962
Nílton Santos	(Brazil)	1958, 1962
Vavá	(Brazil)	1958, 1962
Mário Zagallo	(Brazil)	1958, 1962
Zito	(Brazil)	1958, 1962

LEFT: Italy captain Giuseppe Meazza receives the Jules Rimet trophy in 1938.

FIFA WORLD CUP GOALSCORING RECORDS

The old adage is that "goals win matches" and it is true that most fans want to watch goals being scored. Many FIFA World Cup record-breaking goalscorers become legends overnight, while others enjoy one special moment in the spotlight.

TOP-SCORING TEAM AT EACH FIFA WORLD CUP

YEAR	TEAM	GOALS
1930	Argentina	18 (5 matches)
1934	Italy	12 (5 matches)
1938	Hungary	15 (4 matches)
1950	Brazil	22 (6 matches)
1954	Hungary	27 (5 matches)
1958	France	23 (6 matches)
1962	Brazil	14 (6 matches)
1966	Portugal	17 (6 matches)
1970	Brazil	19 (6 matches)
1974	Poland	16 (7 matches)
1978	Argentina/Netherlands	15 (7 matches)
1982	France	16 (6 matches)
1986	Argentina	14 (7 matches)
1990	West Germany	15 (7 matches)
1994	Sweden	15 (7 matches)
1998	France	15 (7 matches)
2002	Brazil	18 (7 matches)
2006	Germany	14 (7 matches)
2010	Germany	16 (7 matches)
2014	Germany	18 (7 matches)
2018	Belgium	16 (7 matches)

TOTAL GOALS AT EACH FIFA WORLD CUP

YEAR	TOTAL GOALS	TOTAL GAMES	GOALS PER MATCH
1930	70	18	3.89
1934	70	17	4.12
1938	84	18	4.67
1950	88	22	4.00
1954	140	26	5.38
1958	126	35	3.60
1962	89	32	2.78
1966	89	32	2.78
1970	95	32	2.97
1974	97	38	2.55
1978	102	38	2.68
1982	146	52	2.81
1986	132	52	2.54
1990	115	52	2.21
1994	141	52	2.71
1998	171	64	2.67
2002	161	64	2.52
2006	147	64	2.30
2010	145	64	2.27
2014	171	64	2.67
2018	169	64	2.64

BELOW: Miroslav Klose hails Germany's second goal in their semi-final defeat of Brazil in Belo Horizonte.

BIGGEST WINS AT FIFA WORLD CUP FINAL TOURNAMENTS

Hungary 10-1 El Salvador	(1982)
Hungary 9-0 Korea Republic	(1954)
Yugoslavia 9-0 Zaire	(1974)
Sweden 8-0 Cuba	(1938)
Uruguay 8-0 Bolivia	(1950)
Germany 8-0 Saudi Arabia	(2002)
Turkey 7-0 Korea Republic	(1954)
Uruguay 7-0 Scotland	(1954)
Poland 7-0 Haiti	(1974)
Portugal 7-0 Korea DPR	(2010)

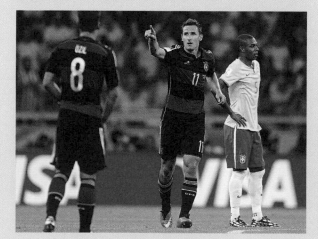

SINGLE-TOURNAMENT TOP SCORERS

NUMBER OF GOALS	GOALSCORER	YEAR
13	Just Fontaine (France)	1958
11	Sándor Kocsis (Hungary)	1954
10	Gerd Müller (West Germany)	1970

PENALTY SHOOT-OUTS BY COUNTRY

NUMBER OF PENALTY SHOOT-OUTS	COUNTRY	RECORD
5	Argentina	(4 wins, 1 defeat)
4	West Germany/ Germany	(4 wins)
4	Brazil	(3 wins, 1 defeat)
4	France	(2 wins, 2 defeats)
4	England	(1 win, 3 defeats)
4	Italy	(1 win, 3 defeats)
4	Spain	(1 win, 3 defeats)
3	Netherlands	(1 win, 2 defeats)
2	Croatia	(2 wins)
2	Republic of Ireland	(1 win, 1 defeat)
2	Costa Rica	(1 win, 1 defeat)
2	Russia	(1 win, 1 defeat)
2	Mexico	(2 defeats)
2	Romania	(2 defeats)
1	16 other nations	

ALL FIFA WORLD CUP FINAL TOURNAMENT TOP SCORERS

YEAR	HOST	NAME (COUNTRY)	NUMBER OF GOALS
1930	(Uruguay)	Guillermo Stábile (Argentina)	8
1934	(Italy)	Oldřich Nejedlý (Czechoslovakia)	5
1938	(France)	Leônidas (Brazil)	7
1950	(Brazil)	Ademir (Brazil)	8
1954	(Switzerland)	Sándor Kocsis (Hungary)	11
1958	(Sweden)	Just Fontaine (France)	13
1962	(Chile)	Garrincha (Brazil)	4
=		Vavá (Brazil)	4
=		Leonel Sánchez (Chile)	4
=		Flórián Albert (Hungary)	4
=		Valentin Ivanov (Soviet Union)	4
=		Dražan Jerković (Yugoslavia)	4
1966	(England)	Eusébio (Portugal)	9
1970	(Mexico)	Gerd Müller (West Germany)	10
1974	(West Germany)	Grzegorz Lato (Poland)	7
1978	(Argentina)	Mario Kempes (Argentina)	6
1982	(Spain)	Paolo Rossi (Italy)	6
1986	(Mexico)	Gary Lineker (England)	6
1990	(Italy)	Salvatore Schillaci (Italy)	6
1994	(USA)	Hristo Stoichkov (Bulgaria)	6
=		Oleg Salenko (Russia)	6
1998	(France)	Davor Šuker (Croatia)	6
2002	(Japan/Korea Republic)	Ronaldo (Brazil)	8
2006	(Germany)	Miroslav Klose (Germany)	5
2010	(South Africa)	Thomas Müller (Germany)	5
=		David Villa (Spain)	5
=		Wesley Sneijder (Netherlands)	5
=		Diego Forlán (Uruguay)	5
2014	(Brazil)	James Rodríguez (Colombia)	6
2018	(Russia)	Harry Kane (England)	6

FIFA WORLD CUP FINAL TOURNAMENT ALL-TIME LEADING GOALSCORERS

GOALS	NAME (COUNTRY)	TOURNAMENTS (MATCHES PLAYED)
16	Miroslav Klose (Germany)	2002, 2006, 2010, 2014 (24)
15	Ronaldo (Brazil)	1998, 2002, 2006 (19)
14	Gerd Müller (West Germany)	1970, 1974 (13)
13	Just Fontaine (France)	1958 (6)
12	Pelé (Brazil)	1958, 1962, 1966, 1970 (14)
11	Sándor Kocsis (Hungary)	1954 (5)
11	Jürgen Klinsmann (West Germany/Germany)	1990, 1994, 1998 (17)
10	Helmut Rahn (West Germany)	1954, 1958 (10)
10	Gary Lineker (England)	1986, 1990 (12)
10	Gabriel Batistuta (Argentina)	1994, 1998, 2002 (12)
10	Teófilo Cubillas (Peru)	1970, 1978, 1982 (13)
10	Thomas Müller (Germany)	2010, 2014, 2018 (16)
10	Grzegorz Lato (Poland)	1974, 1978, 1982 (20)

FIFA WORLD CUP OTHER RECORDS

FIFA WORLD CUP
Qatar2022™

Managing the winning national team at the FIFA World Cup is considered by many to be the greatest possible career achievement for any coach. It is also such a challenge that only one man, Italy's Vittorio Pozzo, has achieved it twice and that was more than 80 years ago.

FIFA WORLD CUP-WINNING COACHES

YEAR	COACH	TEAM
1930	Alberto Suppici	(Uruguay)
1934	Vittorio Pozzo	(Italy)
1938	Vittorio Pozzo	(Italy)
1950	Juan López	(Uruguay)
1954	Sepp Herberger	(West Germany)
1958	Vicente Feola	(Brazil)
1962	Aymoré Moreira	(Brazil)
1966	Alf Ramsey	(England)
1970	Mário Zagallo	(Brazil)
1974	Helmut Schön	(West Germany)
1978	César Luis Menotti	(Argentina)
1982	Enzo Bearzot	(Italy)
1986	Carlos Bilardo	(Argentina)
1990	Franz Beckenbauer	(West Germany)
1994	Carlos Alberto Parreira	(Brazil)
1998	Aimé Jacquet	(France)
2002	Luiz Felipe Scolari	(Brazil)
2006	Marcello Lippi	(Italy)
2010	Vicente del Bosque	(Spain)
2014	Joachim Löw	(Germany)
2018	Didier Deschamps	(France)

FIFA WORLD CUP WINNERS AS PLAYER AND COACH

NAME	AS PLAYER	AS COACH
Mário Zagallo (Brazil)	1958, 1962	1970
Franz Beckenbauer (West Germany)	1974	1990
Didier Deschamps (France)	1998	2018

FIFA WORLD CUP FINAL TOURNAMENT RED CARDS

YEAR	NUMBER OF RED CARDS	YEAR	NUMBER OF RED CARDS
1930	1	1982	5
1934	1	1986	8
1938	4	1990	16
1950	0	1994	15
1954	3	1998	22
1958	3	2002	17
1962	6	2006	28
1966	5	2010	17
1970	0	2014	10
1974	5	2018	4
1978	3		

FASTEST RED CARDS IN FIFA WORLD CUP FINAL TOURNAMENTS

1 min	José Batista (Uruguay) v. Scotland 1986	
3 min	Marco Etcheverry* (Bolivia) v. Germany 1994	
=	Ion Vlădoiu* (Romania) v. Switzerland 1994	
=	Morten Wieghorst* (Denmark) v. South Africa 1998	
4 min	Carlos Sánchez (Colombia) v. Japan 2018	
6 min	Lauren* (Cameroon) v. Chile 1998	
8 min	Giorgio Ferrini (Italy) v. Chile 1962	
=	Miklos Molnar* (Denmark) v. South Africa 1998	

Number of minutes for which players were on the pitch.

* Time on the pitch after entering the game as a substitute.

UNSUCCESSFUL FIFA WORLD CUP HOSTING BIDS

1930	Hungary, Italy, Netherlands, Spain, Sweden
1934	Sweden
1938	Argentina, Germany
1950	None
1954	None
1958	None
1962	Argentina, West Germany
1966	Spain, West Germany
1970	Argentina, Colombia, Japan, Peru
1974	Italy, Netherlands, Spain
1978	Colombia, Mexico
1982	Italy, West Germany
1986	Colombia (won rights but later withdrew), Canada, USA
1990	Austria, England, France, Greece, IR Iran, Soviet Union, West Germany, Yugoslavia
1994	Brazil, Chile, Morocco
1998	England, France, Germany, Morocco, Switzerland
2002	Mexico
2006	Brazil, England, Morocco, South Africa
2010	Egypt, Libya/Tunisia, Morocco
2014	Argentina, Colombia
2018	England, Netherlands/Belgium, Spain/Portugal
2022	USA, Korea Republic, Japan, Australia
2026	Morocco

BIGGEST WINS IN FIFA WORLD CUP QUALIFIERS

1	Australia 31-0 American Samoa 11 April 2001
2	Australia 22-0 Tonga 9 April 2001
3	IR Iran 19-0 Guam 24 November 2000
4	Maldives 0-17 IR Iran 2 June 1997
5	Tajikistan 16-0 Guam 26 November 2000
=	Fiji 16-0 Tuvalu 25 August 2007
7	Qatar 15-0 Bhutan 3 September 2015
=	Vanuatu 15-0 American Samoa 30 August 2007
9	Mongolia 0-14 Japan 30 March 2021
=	IR Iran 14-0 Cambodia 10 October 2019

FIFA WORLD CUP RED AND YELLOW CARDS COMBINED, BY COUNTRY

131	Argentina
120	Germany
115	Brazil

MOST CARDS IN A FIFA WORLD CUP FINAL TOURNAMENT MATCH

20	(4 red and 16 yellow): Portugal v. Netherlands (2006)

QUALIFYING COMPETITION ENTRANTS

HOST(S)	YEAR	NUMBER OF ENTRANTS
Uruguay	1930	(no qualifying competition)
Italy	1934	32
France	1938	37
Brazil	1950	34
Switzerland	1954	45
Sweden	1958	55
Chile	1962	56
England	1966	74
Mexico	1970	75
West Germany	1974	99
Argentina	1978	107
Spain	1982	109
Mexico	1986	121
Italy	1990	116
USA	1994	147
France	1998	174
Japan/Korea Republic	2002	199
Germany	2006	198
South Africa	2010	204
Brazil	2014	207
Russia	2018	209
Qatar	2022	207

FIFA WORLD CUP FINAL REFEREES

YEAR	REFEREE (COUNTRY)
1930	John Langenus (Belgium)
1934	Ivan Eklind (Sweden)
1938	Georges Capdeville (France)
1950	George Reader (England)
1954	William Ling (England)
1958	Maurice Guigue (France)
1962	Nikolay Latyshev (Soviet Union)
1966	Gottfried Dienst (Switzerland)
1970	Rudi Glöckner (West Germany)
1974	Jack Taylor (England)
1978	Sergio Gonella (Italy)
1982	Arnaldo Cézar Coelho (Brazil)
1986	Romualdo Arppi Filho (Brazil)
1990	Edgardo Codesal (Mexico)
1994	Sándor Puhl (Hungary)
1998	Said Belqola (Morocco)
2002	Pierluigi Collina (Italy)
2006	Horacio Elizondo (Argentina)
2010	Howard Webb (England)
2014	Nicola Rizzoli (Italy)
2018	Néstor Pitana (Argentina)

MATCH SCHEDULE AND RESULTS CHART

GROUP A

21 Nov, 13:00	Senegal	0 2	Netherlands	Al Thumama
21 Nov, 19:00	Qatar	0 2	Ecuador	Al Bayt
25 Nov, 16:00	Qatar	1 3	Senegal	Al Thumama
25 Nov, 19:00	Netherlands	1 1	Ecuador	Khalifa International
29 Nov, 19:00	Netherlands	2 0	Qatar	Al Bayt
29 Nov, 19:00	Ecuador	1 2	Senegal	Khalifa International

Team	P	W	D	L	GD	Pts
1. NETHERLANDS	3	2	1	0	+4	7
2. SENEGAL	3	2	0	1	+1	6
3. ECUADOR	3	1	1	1	+1	4
4. QATAR	3	0	0	3	-6	0

GROUP B

21 Nov, 16:00	England	6 2	IR Iran	Khalifa International
21 Nov, 22:00	USA	1 1	Euro play-off	Ahmad Bin Ali
25 Nov, 13:00	Euro play-off	0 2	IR Iran	Ahmad Bin Ali
25 Nov, 22:00	England	0 0	USA	Al Bayt
29 Nov, 22:00	IR Iran	0 1	USA	Al Thumama
29 Nov, 22:00	Euro play-off	0 3	England	Ahmad Bin Ali

Team	P	W	D	L	GD	Pts
1. ENGLAND	3	2	1	0	+7	7
2. USA	3	1	2	0	+1	5
3. IRAN	3	1	0	2	-3	3
4. WALES	3	0	1	2	-5	1

GROUP C

22 Nov, 13:00	Argentina	1 2	Saudi Arabia	Lusail
22 Nov, 19:00	Mexico	0 0	Poland	Stadium 974
26 Nov, 16:00	Poland	2 0	Saudi Arabia	Education City
26 Nov, 22:00	Argentina	2 0	Mexico	Lusail
30 Nov, 22:00	Poland	0 2	Argentina	Stadium 974
30 Nov, 22:00	Saudi Arabia	1 2	Mexico	Lusail

Team	P	W	D	L	GD	Pts
1. ARGENTINA	3	2	0	1	+3	6
2. POLAND	3	1	1	1	0	4
3. MEXICO	3	1	1	1	-1	4
4. SAUDI ARABIA	3	1	0	2	-2	3

GROUP D

22 Nov, 16:00	Denmark	0 0	Tunisia	Education City
22 Nov, 22:00	France	4 1	IC play-off 1	Al Janoub
26 Nov, 13:00	Tunisia	0 1	IC play-off 1	Al Janoub
26 Nov, 19:00	France	2 1	Denmark	Stadium 974
30 Nov, 19:00	IC play-off 1	1 0	Denmark	Al Janoub
30 Nov, 19:00	Tunisia	1 0	France	Education City

Team	P	W	D	L	GD	Pts
1. FRANCE	3	2	0	1	+3	6
2. AUSTRALIA	3	2	0	1	-1	6
3. TUNISIA	3	1	1	1	0	4
4. DENMARK	3	0	1	2	-2	1

GROUP E

23 Nov, 16:00	Germany	1 2	Japan	Khalifa International
23 Nov, 19:00	Spain	7 0	IC play-off 2	Al Thumama
27 Nov, 13:00	Japan	0 1	IC play-off 2	Ahmad Bin Ali
27 Nov, 22:00	Spain	1 1	Germany	Al Bayt
1 Dec, 22:00	Japan	2 1	Spain	Khalifa International
1 Dec, 22:00	IC play-off 2	2 4	Germany	Al Bayt

Team	P	W	D	L	GD	Pts
1. JAPAN	3	2	0	1	+1	6
2. SPAIN	3	1	1	1	+6	4
3. GERMANY	3	1	1	1	+1	4
4. COSTA RICA	3	1	0	2	-8	3

GROUP F

23 Nov, 13:00	Morocco	0 0	Croatia	Al Bayt
23 Nov, 22:00	Belgium	1 0	Canada	Ahmad Bin Ali
27 Nov, 16:00	Belgium	0 2	Morocco	Al Thumama
27 Nov, 19:00	Croatia	4 1	Canada	Khalifa International
1 Dec, 19:00	Croatia	0 0	Belgium	Ahmad Bin Ali
1 Dec, 19:00	Canada	1 2	Morocco	Al Thumama

Team	P	W	D	L	GD	Pts
1. MOROCCO	3	2	1	0	+3	7
2. CROATIA	3	1	2	0	+3	5
3. BELGIUM	3	1	1	1	-1	4
4. CANADA	3	0	0	3	-5	0

GROUP G

24 Nov, 13:00	Switzerland	1	0	Cameroon	Al Janoub
24 Nov, 22:00	Brazil	2	0	Serbia	Lusail
28 Nov, 13:00	Cameroon	3	3	Serbia	Al Janoub
28 Nov, 19:00	Brazil	1	0	Switzerland	Stadium 974
2 Dec, 22:00	Serbia	2	3	Switzerland	Stadium 974
2 Dec, 22:00	Cameroon	1	0	Brazil	Lusail

Team	P	W	D	L	GD	Pts
1. BRAZIL	3	2	0	1	+2	6
2. SWITZERLAND	3	2	0	1	+1	6
3. CAMEROON	3	1	1	1	0	4
4. SERBIA	3	0	1	2	-3	1

GROUP H

24 Nov, 16:00	Uruguay	0	0	Korea Republic	Education City
24 Nov, 19:00	Portugal	3	2	Ghana	Stadium 974
28 Nov, 16:00	Korea Republic	2	3	Ghana	Education City
28 Nov, 22:00	Portugal	2	0	Uruguay	Lusail
2 Dec, 19:00	Ghana	0	2	Uruguay	Al Janoub
2 Dec, 19:00	Korea Republic	2	1	Portugal	Education City

Team	P	W	D	L	GD	Pts
1. PORTUGAL	3	2	0	1	+2	6
2. SOUTH KOREA	3	1	1	1	0	4
3. URUGUAY	3	1	1	1	0	4
4. GHANA	3	1	0	2	-2	3

ROUND OF 16

3 Dec, 19:00	NETHERLANDS	◇	◇	USA	Khalifa International Stadium
3 Dec, 22:00	ARGENTINA	◇	◇	AUSTRALIA	Ahmad Bin Ali Stadium
4 Dec, 22:00	ENGLAND	◇	◇	SENEGAL	Al Bayt Stadium
4 Dec, 19:00	FRANCE	◇	◇	POLAND	Al Thumama Stadium
5 Dec, 19:00	JAPAN	◇	◇	CROATIA	Al Janoub Stadium
5 Dec, 22:00	BRAZIL	◇	◇	SOUTH KOREA	Stadium 947
6 Dec, 19:00	MOROCCO	◇	◇	SPAIN	Education City Stadium
6 Dec, 22:00	PORTUGAL	◇	◇	SWITZERLAND	Lusail Stadium

QUARTER-FINALS

9 Dec, 22:00	Winner 1	◇	◇	Winner 2	Lusail Stadium
9 Dec, 19:00	Winner 5	◇	◇	Winner 6	Education City Stadium
10 Dec, 22:00	Winner 3	◇	◇	Winner 4	Al Bayt Stadium
10 Dec, 19:00	Winner 7	◇	◇	Winner 8	Al Thumama Stadium

SEMI-FINALS

| 13 Dec, 22:00 | Winner QF1 | ◇ | ◇ | Winner QF2 | Lusail Stadium |
| 14 Dec, 22:00 | Winner QF3 | ◇ | ◇ | Winner QF4 | Al Bayt Stadium |

THIRD-PLACE PLAY-OFF

| 17 Dec, 19:00 | Loser SF1 | ◇ | ◇ | Loser SF2 | Khalifa International Stadium |

FIFA WORLD CUP 2022 FINAL

| 18 Dec, 19:00 | Winner SF1 | ◇ | ◇ | Winner SF2 | Lusail Stadium |

FIFA WORLD CUP Qatar2022™

PICTURE CREDITS

The publishers would like to thank the following sources for their kind permission to reproduce the pictures in this book. (T-top, B-bottom, L-left, R-right)